Your
DESIRED
Future

ALSO BY HENRY CLOUD

Trust: Knowing When to Give It, When to Withhold It

Necessary Endings: The Employees, Businesses, and Relationships That All of Us Have to Give Up in Order to Move Forward

Boundaries for Leaders: Results, Relationships, and Being Ridiculously in Charge

The Power of the Other: The Startling Effect Other People Have on You, from the Boardroom to the Bedroom and Beyond— and What to Do About It

Integrity: The Courage to Meet the Demands of Reality

Boundaries: When to Say Yes, How to Say No to Take Control of Your Life

Changes That Heal: Four Practical Steps to a Happier, Healthier You

Why I Believe: A Psychologist's Thoughts on Suffering, Miracles, Science and Faith

Your DESIRED Future

THE 5 ESSENTIAL STEPS THAT TAKE YOU WHERE YOU WANT TO GO

DR. HENRY CLOUD

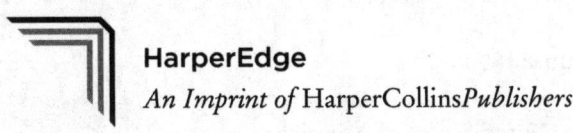

HarperEdge

An Imprint of HarperCollins*Publishers*

HarperCollins books may be purchased for educational, business, or sales promotional use. For information, please email the Special Markets Department at SPsales@harpercollins.com.

hc.com

FIRST EDITION

Library of Congress Cataloging-in-Publication Data has been applied for.

ISBN 978-0-06-348783-3

Printed in the United States of America

26 27 28 29 30 LBC 5 4 3 2 1

This book is dedicated to my incredible clients over the years. Your passion, talents, and diligence have inspired me and taught me. It has been an incredible privilege to work alongside you. You have shown time and time again, the truth of these concepts.

"When you know where you want to go, it's helpful to have a clear path to get there."

—Dr. Henry Cloud

Contents

Your
DESIRED
Future

Your Desired Future May Be Closer Than You Think

I love our family dog, Finley. She is a Doberman and extremely smart and gifted. I have always loved big working breeds, having raised and trained five German shepherds, a Rottweiler/Doberman, and now Fin. I love them because they are extremely loving (we refer to Finley as Velcro since she loves to glue herself to you to express her affection). But they are also very task-oriented. They get things done. If well trained, they accomplish their mission.

Part of Finley's mission is to play a specific role by not only adding to the love in the family and providing much humor, but also making sure that we are safe and secure. She guards the perimeter of our home. Much like any good boundary guard, she lets the good stuff in and keeps the bad stuff out. When someone arrives at the front door, she races to it and stops them from entering until she can determine whether they are friend or foe.

If she knows they are a friend, her ears go back, and her scary bark becomes welcoming. If it's the other way around and she sees a stranger, her bark warns, "Stop! . . . awaiting further instructions." Then one of us will go to the door and let her know if this is a friend, a stranger, or some other danger. She does a great job.

But there is a drawback, even to great breeds. Finley executes her mission only in the way that she has been wired, instinctually, and through her training. She just does what she is wired and programmed to do. But I have *never* seen her bark, pause, sit back, and ask herself, "I wonder if that was helpful? Did I bark at the right time? Loud enough? Too loud?" Nor the bigger question for us in this book, "Will that bark help me get to where I want to be on Thursday?" That's never happened. She never gets *above her habitual behavior* to *observe, evaluate, and organize it towards a better end.*

That ability is pretty much reserved for the human species. While Finley is not thinking about next Thursday, we *do* have that capacity. Only humans are designed to imagine a *desired future state* and *organize energy and activities to make that desire come to fruition.* To make it actually happen in the real world. To make our lives and the lives of others better. To get *there* from the *here* that we possess today. In life and leadership, we call that future a vision.

But too many times, for all of us, the desired futures we imagine and plan never materialize. Sometimes, this can certainly be for reasons outside of our control. Either forces majeure or bad people can prohibit some visions from materializing. But the truth is, many times our desired future dreams and goals are *not* prevented by circumstances outside of our control. We labor, work hard, try our best—at least it feels like we do, and yet somehow still don't get *there*. We have the talent and the brains or the opportunity that is needed, and yet, six months later, a year, or even longer, it still hasn't happened. You might have felt that in one of these ways:

- A business or a business initiative that didn't make it
- A health goal that you didn't reach
- A revenue goal that wasn't achieved
- A relationship that didn't improve or even failed
- A dream that never got off the ground
- Profits that never materialized
- The book you always wanted to write that only remains a great idea in your head
- A team that never seems able to come together to produce the results it should

We could go on and on, probably just by reviewing our own histories, but no need to do that. You get the idea, and there is no need to wallow in our misses. We all know what it feels like. As the proverb says, "Hope deferred makes the heart sick, but a desire fulfilled is a tree of life" (Prov. 13:12).

If the reasons we don't get there aren't outside of our control, why does it happen, even when we might have the abilities to get there? And more to the point of this book, is there something *within our control* that we can do to help ensure better outcomes? Better than we have gotten in the past or are getting in the present? Even more to the point, is there a *specific* way we can engage our time, energies, and talents to give ourselves the best shot at getting *there*?

Yes, there is. There is a way. While Finley's chances of getting to a desired future on Thursday largely depend upon things outside of her control—her caretakers, her trainers, and her environment—yours are not limited by your species. Your chances of getting *there* are empowered by the design of being a human. You have a different brain than Finley does. *You have the ability to organize your efforts in the* way *or the* path *from here to there; it's a universal way that virtually everything, large and small, gets done.* We really do know, from performance research and neuroscience, how humans and their goals advance from one place to a desired, decided upon, and nonexistent new reality. There truly is a way that it virtually always happens.

Having had the privilege and blessing of working with many high performers for over three decades, I have seen people realize extraordinary achievements. From building global companies, turning failing entities around, improving business cultures and performance, to overcoming the most daunting of personal challenges in terms of clinical issues, relationship nightmares, and personal foibles. I have seen what seemed impossible be achieved. At the same time, I have seen many who *don't* get *there. What's startling is that there is not a lot of difference in the brains and talents of those who do, and those who don't.* That is not where the difference usually lies.

Certainly, in the extreme outliers of performance, there are those whose talents and X factors are in a league of their own. I am a lifelong competitive golfer, but I will never be Tiger Woods. I am not saying that if you know the *way* things get done, you can be as good as anyone else who tries it. There are super-gifted people who surpass nearly everyone. But *in most endeavors, people do possess the intellect and other faculties that are needed for success when they are in their arena.* In the raw material, they are not defective or deficient, although their failures sometimes make them feel that way. The problem is *not* that they are not Tiger. *The problem is usually that they do not go about their endeavors in the way that success and good results are achieved.* And then, as I have seen many times when they do, the results come.

And to my main point, when they do get to their particular *there*, they followed the same path that those extraordinary outliers did. I will never be Tiger. His scores will be better than mine for sure. But to get *my* best scores will require my following the same path as Tiger. *There is a way forward from which success follows.*

For a plane to stay in the air, it must be flown in accordance with the laws of physics. Similarly, there are laws that govern solving difficult problems and achieving a vision from scratch. The path is the same and contains essential elements, whether making and executing something "better" or creating a tangible successful reality that does not yet even exist. There is a way that it is done.

In this book, we will look at the elements of that universal path and how you can align your energies and your activities with it to increase your odds of success.

There are three lenses that we shall look through together along this journey. First, we will learn the path itself, the way you must travel from here to your desired future state. By spending decades in the study of the science of performance as well as in war rooms with businesses and individuals—from industry to professional sports to nonprofits—I have seen there are five essential steps that must always be present and executed.

Likewise, when people don't get *there*, there is almost always at least one factor that was missed, not given attention, not known about, or faulty in their execution. So, we will do a deep dive into understanding what the five essential steps are and how to execute them.

Good news: They are not rocket science. Just like a kid throwing a Frisbee and a space shuttle hurtling into outer space, both deal with the same laws of physics. You just have to order your activities in a way that keeps your vision airborne, no matter what its size or complexity. Yes, losing thirty pounds might be "simpler" than running a global enterprise, but the laws of achievement are the same for both tasks. You can learn them. They are simple, but profound in their demanding requirements and their promise of results.

A second lens will also require you to do some personal work. The harsh reality is that none of us naturally possesses all five of the elements we will see are necessary for success. You are better at a few than I am, and I might be better than you at a couple of others. But even though we are not good at all of them, *we both must make sure they are all present in our endeavors, both personal and professional*. The harsh truth is that many times, we are like Finley. We tackle the vision in the way that we are wired. We instinctively try to *get there*. So, naturally, we do a few of the five better than the others, *but the goal requires all five*. As I say to leaders often, "You are building your company [or your team or department] in your own image . . . with the same strengths and deficits that you have." Their companies or departments or paths of achievement look like them, with their same strengths and weaknesses.

More good news: Your weaknesses don't have to become equal

to your strengths. You just have to make sure those essentials are given their due in other ways. (More about that later!)

Is it possible that you have been acting more like Finley than you care to admit? Maybe you've never even asked the crucial question that Finley omits, the question of self-observation: "Will the way I am doing this get me closer to where I want to be on Thursday?" Said another way, we often don't naturally get above our work and efforts to observe them. We just bark and charge the door in the way that we know how and are wired to do, through a combination of nature and nurture. We just try our best and go for it. And sometimes, the necessary moment to stop and ask "Am I doing what is universally required to get to my desired Thursday?" doesn't happen. In a sense, we play the game in the ways we are constructed, and often, *we don't know what we don't know about what is required and may be missing from the picture.*

I will help you take a look at how you are trying to get there to identify which of the five essentials may be missing or may not come naturally to you without some self-observation, and, might I add, *growth*. This book not only provides the necessary technical, actionable advice, but it also encourages you to reflect about yourself, to identify how you are trying to get there and what may need a tweak or two. As a psychologist and a coach, I intend to push you towards a few growth steps when needed.

And third, while the five essentials sound simple, each requires specific activities and methods. We need to learn them and get good at them. It is not hard . . . it's just *hard* . . . if you know what that means. As with learning to ride a bike, it's not hard, but it does take focus and effort, and it can feel hard at the beginning. But it's doable, of that I can assure you. I will try to make it as simple for you as possible.

So, I want you to have two big takeaways from this chapter. First, you don't have to feel like a failure or like you are defective in some way if some of your desired futures have not been achieved. You probably are very gifted and talented; it's probably just that you're skipping one or two of these essentials, or not executing them properly. That is fixable! I see people do it every day.

Second, now that you know that you are not defective or a loser, you can enter into whatever your endeavor is, not only with hope, but also with hope that doesn't have to be deferred. I will show you how to get started on the path to your desired future now. I want you to have a simple GPS map, a navigational tool that you can check on to make sure you are on track to making your *there* a reality. No one drives without a map and instrument gauges. This book will provide you with that.

There are a lot of ways to hit a perfect golf shot, but no matter your style or particular flavor of swinging the club, essential elements must be present, such as the club must finally approach the ball on a certain line with a square face and speed. No matter what your swing looks like, the essentials must be met, and you can take great hope once you learn what those are and do them in your own way. While Bill Gates and Steve Jobs were very different in their styles and approaches to creating a desired future state (one that we all now live in and enjoy every day), they both lived out the five elements we will learn here. That is what this book is about. So, let's get to it.

CHAPTER 2

Your Body Knows Best

Jared was bummed. And as CEO, his way of being *bummed* was not *down-in-the-mouth depressed*. When he is not happy, it comes out more like an agitated energy. When he entered a room for a meeting with his team, everyone knew he was not happy. He doesn't hide it well, not that he even tries. And when Jared isn't happy, *ain't nobody happy* around that building.

The group at this meeting was on alert, knowing that this once highly successful business unit, which had previously achieved phenomenal year-over-year growth, had now stalled. And worse than that, it was Jared's favorite business unit of the entire enterprise. It was his pride and joy, and it was flat for the second year in a row. The team knew that this was not going to be a happy meeting.

I met Jared through a joint venture I was consulting on, where he was a stakeholder, and he was familiar with my work with teams. When he called me and asked if I would work with his executive team as they tackled their business challenges, I was excited to do it as he is such a brilliant leader, and I love the business they are in. He said he would organize an off-site with his senior leadership team, where I, as their facilitator, would help them take a deeper look at why this once-thriving business had plateaued. Since the market still had great demand and their product was very good, it made no sense for it to have flattened. Jared wanted to find the answer. From the briefing he'd given me, I was almost certain that the answer was a leadership issue. The team was running the business unit, but obviously not in a way that could sustain their previous success.

After introductions to the team and understanding the VPs' roles, I began with a simple assignment. I gave them all three-by-five cards and told them, "You all are the leaders of this business. You are leading it to your vision and goals. So, I want you to silently answer this question and write the answer down on the card." The question I asked them was:

What does leadership do to make something
get from where it is to where you want it to be?
Asked another way, "What is leadership?"

They went to work and handed me their cards. *The result was that I got seven different answers as to what leadership is supposed to be doing.* To their credit, all of them were "good" answers, having real value, but at the same time, they were all *different*. What that told me was that the team had no agreement about what they as leaders of the business were supposed to be doing to reach their goal. That was the heart of the problem. They would never be able to lead their team to it if they didn't agree on what leadership meant and how to get there.

They lacked a clear path, a GPS map to help them get this business from here (stagnant) to there (winning).

That map, that path, that way is what this chapter and this book are about.

Finding the Path

I was trained as a clinical psychologist. Clinical psychologists help people in three big areas. First, we help with clinical issues such as moods, thinking, anxieties, addictions, fears, and the like. Second, we address relational issues that arise in all areas of life, such as marriage, parenting, work, dating, and so on. And third, we help with performance issues, such as finding one's goals and reaching them. This has been and continues to be my life's work in many contexts.

When I went knocking on doors looking for a job as a young clinician, a leadership consulting firm hired me to help business leaders whose "personal" issues were interfering with their leadership and organizational performance. Said another way, "who they were" was getting in the way of "what they were trying to accomplish." I fell in love with working with high-performing and talented people who were working on important missions in their personal lives and businesses. And I fell in love with the field of leadership, which allowed me to bring together all three areas of clinical psychology into my approach when working with leaders and their teams.

What I saw over and over was exactly what Jared's team was experiencing—very talented and smart people who were, for some reason, not getting there. Many times, there was no lack of talent or knowledge, opportunity, or brains, but things were not working. People were either falling short of what they dreamed of, or worse, ending up badly broken and even causing harm.

Over the years, a pattern became clear to me. When you take away external business challenges, such as bad markets, interest rate issues, supply-chain challenges, and the like, or personal obstacles such as trauma or other difficult circumstances, the reason individuals, teams, and businesses get stuck is because *something is lacking in the way they are trying to get there.*

Remember Finley never getting to a better Thursday? In the same way, you and your team may be working hard, but success remains stubborn and elusive. It's like the bow wave of a boat. You can never quite catch it, never quite get there.

Sometimes it's caused by a bad leader or personal dysfunction. It might be due to the personal makeup of a key person or due to a complete lack of leadership. Other times, it just seems "unknowable" but continuously disappointing.

Either way, it usually adds up to a lot of activity that goes nowhere—a lot of energy expended without forward motion.

After many years of seeing this pattern repeated over and over, I found myself longing for a simple model that I could give to people to help them quickly diagnose what was missing or what was broken—and then set a productive course to navigate towards the future. I was looking for a model that would help them reach solutions quickly, a model that would help Jared's team get on the same page and generate forward motion. I wanted to give Jared and leaders like him a proven model that encompassed the crucial elements that lead to high performance.

I began to see the need for a model that asked the crucial question: *What does this endeavor need that I am not naturally seeing?* So I went on a quest, scouring the performance and leadership literature and reviewing practical tools to see if a simple model emerged that could get anyone from "here to there." Was there a way that it all hung together that would be profound yet simple, and actionable for everyone?

My search continued. And one day it dawned on me to look at the best model of achievement, performance, and "getting from here to there" that exists: *the human body.* There has never been an achievement machine like it. Nothing comes close to its complex interworking and systems that, taken together, accomplish a myriad of different and remarkable endeavors. So, I decided to ask the question: *How does a human body, this amazing performance machine, reach its goals?*

It might sound cheesy, or even simplistic, to look at business and performance that way, but what I found was mindboggling, and encapsulated virtually everything that all leadership and performance literature, books, and content talk about. Let me walk you through what I found and then show you how it applies to reaching your desired future.

The human body's performance center, its "leadership C-suite," is the brain. But unlike Finley's brain, the human brain has the capacity to do much more than just what it is automatically wired to do. While Finley's intelligence is high for dogs, she doesn't have the leadership C-suite to *define a desired future and organize all her activities to make sure her desired Thursday actually comes about.* But *your* human brain does. So, let's let it teach us the best way to get from here to there that has ever been designed. How does the human body get from here to there? Asking this question and then applying it to the kind of problems Jared's team experienced gave me deep insight into what the path looks like.

How the Human Body Gets From *Here* to *There*

If we think of getting from *here* to *there*, we should start by looking at what the body does *first*. It first gets awareness of its present *here* and slowly or quickly concludes that being *here* is not its greatest desire.

Take this example: If you are speaking to an audience in a roomful of people and are standing way over to one side of the room, the first thing your brain does is realize that standing *here* is not the best way to be heard. It says to itself, "I could speak to this group way better if I were standing over *there*." It envisions a better place where it could be, a *there* that it desires.

In the leadership and performance world, we call this a vision. I call it a "desired future state." It's somewhere you really desire to be but have not yet reached. As we shall see, this is very different than Finley following an impulse to be across the room because she sees something over there that she wants. Instead, this is a creative and intentional process to reach for something that can't even be seen and that may not even exist yet. Your heart and your brain *create* a more desirable future. This is the first step on the path.

FIRST: ENVISION THE FUTURE REALITY YOU DESIRE

Once that desired future is clear, it's time for the brain to go there. *So, let's go, brain.* One problem: *The brain is not going anywhere by itself.* It is stuck in its box, sitting on top of the shoulders, unable to go anywhere by itself. Totally stuck until it does its magic.

By activating tens of billions of neurons and the hierarchical networks they are organized into, it immediately begins doing the second big step in getting from here to there: *It engages the talent it is going to need to get there.* The brain is going nowhere by itself. It immediately asks the crucial question: *Who is going to get me over there?* It figures out the specific talent it is going to need to get there and then sends out impulses to recruit that talent and engage it in the process of getting there.

Effectively, it says, "I am going to need a couple of legs to get moving. A set of eyes to focus on where I am going. An inner ear to keep me balanced. A heart to send some oxygenated blood to the equipment," and so forth. It then immediately sends out recruiting impulses to bring that talent on board. Then once it has recruited the talent it will need, it engages all those players in the task, keeping them engaged, motivated, moving, and so on.

The amazing element directs how the human body immediately and seamlessly accomplishes this task. Originating from the leader, the brain's CEO (otherwise known as the prefrontal cortex), who created the vision, the memo then goes out to bring together a team of the necessary talents and resources. These make up the team the brain is going to need to get it to its desired future—its *there*. We will learn much about engaging talent in this book later, but for now just notice one thing: *The brain cannot get there by itself* (hint: neither can you). It is going to need to find the right talent to take it there. This is the second step.

SECOND: ENGAGE THE NECESSARY TALENT

Remember: Engaging talent is a twofold process. First, it asks the question: What talent (abilities) are necessary to get us *there*? Second, it asks: Who are the *individuals* we will put in those positions? Name the talent needed in those positions first, and then fill those roles with people who possess those specific skills and talents. Do not just fill positions with people who are already available or most accessible.

Once the brain gets the talent on board, it does not just take off to get across the room. That would be impulsive, Finley-like behavior. Before it ever gets the team of talent moving, it asks a crucial question: *How am I going to get* there? Think about it. There are a myriad of ways to get across the room. How about calling an Uber? No, it doesn't really fit the context. How about riding a bike? No, the distance doesn't justify the investment. Maybe roll across the floor? No, not necessary, and I'll lose speed and eye contact. Finally, the answer emerges, "I think I'll walk."

At this point, what the brain is doing is answering a crucial question: *How am I going to win?* How am I going to get *there*? In leadership and business parlance, we call this a strategy. The strategy is the key to figuring out the way that you are going to get there. It distinguishes those who get there from those who don't in several ways, but most specifically in that they have an actionable, set course that fits the context to give them the best chance of success. Now we're reached the third step.

THIRD: DEVELOP A STRATEGY AND BUILD A PLAN TO EXECUTE THE STRATEGY

A good strategy also protects against wasted energy and useless activity. Without a strategy, the body would just jump into action, and a lot could go wrong, be wasted, or lead in the wrong direction. I am sure you have seen this in real life as people try to reach their goals.

Within milliseconds, the CEO brain has calculated something else that makes the strategy workable: the plan. *The plan is the railway of the strategy.* It makes the strategy come to life by specifically figuring out three things:

1. What specific activities must be done for the strategy to work?
2. Who is going to do them?
3. When will they do the *what*?

The brain has also figured out a timeline for all of this to happen. It has estimated that it should take you about ten steps to get across the room at one step per second, in a particular direction. It knows where you are headed, how long it should take you, which part of your body must do what, by when.

Now that the body is ready to go—it has a vision, it has the right talent in place, and it has a strategy—it's time to rock and roll. Let's go, right?

Wait . . . not so fast! You might not have noticed this, but before the body starts to take off across the room, something has already taken place. It is wired with a measurement and accountability system that *will make sure it is getting to where it needs to get.* The body is watching and *measuring* itself. It is monitoring itself according to the plan of the strategy. It knows that it is supposed to be walking in a certain direction at a certain speed with a certain number of steps, and it is continuously observing itself to make sure of one thing: *It is doing what it said it was going to do.* This is the essence of accountability—and the fourth step on the path to your desired future.

FOURTH: DEVELOP A *MEASUREMENT* AND *ACCOUNTABILITY* SYSTEM

As we shall see, accountability is not police work, but partner work. It is not like a cop writing a ticket when someone does not do something right, but rather people working together systematically, helping one another reach the goal. It is the ongoing observational system of the body that monitors behavior to ensure its action matches its vision and aligns with the strategy. And the human body does all of this without us even being conscious of it. We will delve deeply into how accountability works in later chapters, but it is one of the most important functions of the human body.

Now the body is really on the move. It is walking across the room to reach its vision of getting "there." Things are happening. But . . . as expected in life, it gets distracted and drifts off course a bit. Someone in the front row asks a question as the speaker is walking to *there.* So, our speaker slows down and turns a few feet to the right, stops and starts to answer the question. Innocent enough . . . but after about ten seconds, something happens. The measurement and accountability system of the human brain sends a message, and gets his attention, saying, "Hey, you need to get back on track and keep walking, or you will not get *there* to be able to speak to the whole room before time runs out." It quickly alerts the system and adjusts based on what the measurement and accountability system finds. It sends impulses to correct and get back on plan. We've reached the fifth and final step in the path.

FIFTH: FIX, ADAPT, AND COURSE CORRECT WHEN PROBLEMS ARE ENCOUNTERED

Bodies who get *there* measure where they are and whether they are doing what they said they would do. When they are off the path, they quickly fix the problem and adapt in a way that gets them back on track. As we shall see in depth later, a problem is normal and meant to be solved. But if it is not quickly solved and repeats or continues, it is no longer a problem. It has become a *pattern*. It has become a mutation in the strategy and will change the entire outcome. Problems get solved; patterns that aren't addressed create failure.

The Five Components

Now you have a preview of the five components we will examine in detail in the rest of this book. They apply to the miraculous system of the human body, but they can also be applied to your personal goals, your work as a leader or team member, and your role as a spouse or parent.

When I overlay these concepts with the literature of leadership and high performance, it is astounding. All that literature is so important to learn. Leadership and performance are sciences, and I always encourage leaders to be avid leadership students. Read all you can to develop leadership and performance skills. We need to know it. But what was astounding to me is that most of that literature tends to look at each of these five in isolation—not as an integrative system where all five elements must be present.

We need books on vision, engaging talent, strategy and execution, accountability, and adapting. We need to go deep into those subjects, which we'll do in the pages that follow. But we will go beyond that to see that to get from where you are to the desired future you envision, you must embrace and invest equally in each of the five components. Failure comes when one or more of these elements are omitted.

And as I've noted, one challenge in becoming a leader is that we tend to build things in our own image. Our businesses, plans, and even our teams and departments tend to look a lot like us, repeating our strengths and weaknesses, which are also evident in our best-laid plans and efforts. For example, you might be great on vision and strategy, but weak on what feels like the boring or conflict-ridden practice of accountability. Without meaning to, you might avoid elements that don't reflect your particular strengths. The result? Teams and organizations built in our own image that fall off track in our here-to-there journey. No worries; no one is strong in every area. But . . . the message of this book is that if you are aware of the five elements that are absolutely necessary, you can make sure they are all being added and done, at least by someone on your team or in your life, even if you might naturally overlook them or not do them well yourself.

You do not have to have all the strengths called for in these five elements. But your business or your life goal does need people to contribute to them all. Even if you personally don't do each of the steps, you must make sure all of them are present and accounted for before you set off on your path. And the best news is that many of those so-called weaknesses are areas of human functioning that you can grow into and get better at. Even if we do not possess them as signature strengths, we can still grow in really helpful ways. Just because you are a bit conflict-avoidant, making you weak on accountability, doesn't mean you can't benefit from learning to have a difficult conversation! I have seen it happen many times. Personal growth in areas you thought you just didn't possess can be extremely rewarding and get you closer to your goals. You might not ever want to be a trial litigator, but you can finally talk to someone about poor performance! Much more about that later.

So as we move forward from here, my goal is for you to get a firm grasp on the five essentials needed to get from here to there, and make sure you are executing them and working on the issues that might be keeping you from doing that.

Back to Jared

The offsite with Jared's team began with a little bit of a startle when I asked them to answer the question: What is leadership? I think they felt a little embarrassed when it became apparent how scattered they were, but we quickly got over that. The next forty-five minutes or so were spent sharing with them the five components and putting five columns up on the whiteboard. From there, we spent time in each column, with the team asking themselves the hard questions about each component.

1. Your Desired Future (Vision)
- What exactly were they trying to achieve? What was their specific *there*?
- How desirable or compelling was that future? Was it desirable and compelling enough to get people to sacrifice for it?

What would it mean for them or others that would make it worth it?

- Had that really been driven and communicated clearly and continuously?
- Was it specific enough?
- Did they actually believe it was possible?
- Did everyone own it and love it?
- What had been missing in the vision and its communication?

2. Engage Talent: Positions and People

- Was everyone clear on what specific talent (skills, expertise, abilities) was needed to get the business where they wanted?
- Did everyone understand their roles? Did the roles reflect the needed talent?
- Having named the needed talent, what talent was missing in this picture? What positions? What expertise?
- Did that needed talent live in the building? Did they need to go outside for that expertise?
- Was a new hire or a consultant required?
- Were the people in place now actually delivering the talent that was needed from the seats they were filling?
- If not, was it something that could be learned or fixed?
- Who should be let go?

3. Strategy/Plan: How Are We Going to Win?

- Did they have a clear strategy, with specific strategic anchors, that would guide all their efforts? Had they answered the question: *How are we going to win?*

- Is the strategy aligned with the business they are really in? Does it fit their core mission?
- Were there multiple strategies? If so, was this a problem? Were they conflicting?
- Were multiple "good" strategies draining resources from the best one?
- Does the current strategy fit the market today as it did in the past? What has changed?
- Have they defined the very specific activities that the execution of the strategy depends upon? Do those drive results?
- Regarding the activities needed to get *there*, is it clear who is to do what and when? Are activities, roles, and timelines very, very clear?

4. Measurement/Accountability

- Have they identified the most important measures they need to know to determine whether they are doing what they said they would do?
- Is what they are measuring directly linked to a result they hope to achieve? Why is each measure relevant?
- Is the measurement system only looking at progress towards a goal? Or is it also actually measuring the *specific activities* that will make it possible to reach the goal?
- Have the accountable parties mutually agreed upon the expectations placed on each of them? Have they agreed on what is being measured and signed off on their responsibility in the accountability relationship? Do they agree on what it will mean to have met the expectations?

- Have the parties agreed upon when they will inspect the measures? What will their cadence be? How often will progress be measured? And in what format (e.g., in-person meetings, e-mail, 1:1, etc.)?
- Have they discussed "what then"? Said another way, have they discussed what will occur if the measurement shows that "we did not do what we said we would do"? What are the next steps and/or consequences then?
- If there is something not being performed as promised, did you ask, "Why didn't this happen as promised?" Or did you just make a commitment to "do it better next time" without solving the potential root cause?
- If measurement and accountability show that you are doing everything just as you said you would, are you getting the results you expected? If so, what will you do with that information? If not, might that mean that you have a strategy problem if you are executing perfectly and not getting *there*?

5. Fix and Adapt

- What happens when a measurement or accountability system reveals that something is broken or not performing?
- Is it clear who is to take what steps when that is the case? Does this happen quickly?
- Was the fix communicated in a way that encourages learning?
- Who owns the fix? Were new skills, training, or help needed?
- What is the communication path to let everyone know who can do something about it if there is a problem?
- Has a timeline been established for implementing the steps to make the fix? Is it clear who is to do what to make the fix?

- Was it a performance problem or strategy problem? Was it a talent problem?
- How will we know when the fix has taken place?
- Do they see how the fix can be moved to the lowest levels to the people who can do it and see it first?
- How will you ensure this won't happen again?

Bringing It All Together

As you can imagine, this exercise went deep into investigating the practices, patterns, activities, and capabilities of team members to be sure that the team had coverage for each step. It was hard work, but it was also energizing and revealing, and brought new hope and direction to Jared's team.

They found the real reasons why his very smart, talented, and experienced team was not experiencing success, even with a great product in a robust market. And all that hope turned into a newfound purpose and direction that brought the team into a new season of getting *there* with great results, and ultimately to a new and improved business model. They learned that their vision had become diluted and wasn't being driven well, having been in place for so many years. People just kind of assumed it worked, rather than pressing harder to see if it still held up to the realities of the market and then fixing and adapting it based on new information. And, they learned that there were some significant missing pieces in how and what they needed to get from here to there. When they returned to that *way*, they began to get *there*.

Some talent had to be added, and some people had to be moved out of the division. And while their basic strategy remained the same, changes in the delivery systems of that strategy needed overhauling, and they did that along with rewriting the plan. They changed their measurement system to get closer to watching the real activities that moved the needle, instead of only looking at results and outcomes. And in terms of fixes, they found many areas where problems were allowed to linger, becoming stubborn patterns that hurt performance. By looking at all five components, they were able to uncover why their great product was not crushing it, as it had in the past.

They also found out that they had not drifted into being losers but were still very good at what they did. They had just begun to drift away from some essential components, such as the right kind of measurement and accountability, which needed specific kinds of attention. In other words, they needed to look at their barking.

While becoming proficient in each component is critical, it's when you put all five together that the path to your desired future state becomes clear and attainable. This five-step path is essential, regardless of the kind of goal or endeavor you attempt. Said another way, no one gets from *here* to *there* without these elements. Whether you are a start-up or an existing business, small or large, trying to resolve a personal issue like depression or weight loss, or even repairing a hurting relationship, these five essential components must be addressed.

1. Where am I now, and where do I desire to go?
2. What talent outside of myself is needed to make it possible?
3. How will I win? What is my strategy and plan to organize my energy?

4. How will I know I am getting there and doing what is needed?
5. Am I fixing what's not working as soon as I find it?

What a marvel the human body is—the way it all works together to produce action and results. It is amazingly complex, yet efficient at the same time. Nothing is ever wasted as the body aligns with what the brain has given its attention to. The neuroscience I will share shows how astounding the human body is at getting there. The parts truly help each other to play their individual roles. For example, if a strategic move is taken that is not part of the vision of getting to the specific *there*, and could potentially have you end up on the wrong side of the room or slow your progress down, the legs pause and say, "Wait . . . get in line . . ." This is thanks to the measurement and accountability system. This type of correction can happen in so many ways as different parts of the body work together.

The great news about this for teams and groups of people going towards a goal together is the unity and energetic oneness that emerges as the parts start working together. It is the essence of genuine team building without cheesy trust falls or having to go bowling or perform some other forced, fun exercises. Like the human body, great teams really are more than the sum of their parts.

The five-step path can also be used to unify a personal support group working together to help each other reach their individual personal goals. The incredible benefit that works its magic is metaphorically not far off from what the Swiss psychiatrist Carl Jung called "synchronicity." That is when you also get phenomena occurring together without direct cause and effect, but because there is a "collective unconscious" that integrates them. The human body, as an operating system, does that, and when we organize our efforts towards a collective *there* with these same components, individual moves create an efficient beauty, like the body of a ballet dancer twirling across a stage.

Imagine your goals being reached through that kind of balanced wholeness of effort, as opposed to constant pushing and shoving to make things happen. It is what other performance researchers call "flow." Everything just comes together. That's what I want for you.

CHAPTER 3

Vision: Can You See It?

Yes, you can. All you need is your eyes. You can see a computer on your desk at home and at work as well. But, if it were the mid 1970s you could walk throughout your entire house, office, or company and not see one computer on a desk. In fact, to see a computer at all, you would have to go to some institution or enterprise where it might be tucked away in a special room.

But if you were Bill Gates, you could *see* a computer on your desk, at home and at work. Yet, you would not be using your eyes, at least your physical ones. You would be using another set of eyes that your body provides, eyes that Finley doesn't quite have. To see your vision, you use eyes that are activated in the default mode network of your brain . . . and probably deep in your metaphorical heart and spirit as well.

That is what Gates did. He saw a future state when every desk would have a computer, readily available for the ordinary person to use. It is called a *vision*. At the time, it was considered a really out-there kind of fantasy. Today, we take it for granted as a reality and might even wonder if something might be wrong if a home or office is without one. What was once a nonexistent desired future state is now everyday *reality*. That is the power of vision. The very first thing your body does to get you from *here* to *there* is to create a vision. And it is the first component of the path for how anything gets done. It is the essential beginning to every outcome, simple and complex, and every accomplishment—from desiring a sandwich from the refrigerator to end hunger pangs, to creating a new business. It is the ability to see something that does not yet exist, something desired so strongly that it motivates one to take action to turn that desire into reality. Without it, everything is just a fantasy. Does Finley have fantasies of one day owning her own house full of rib-eye steaks? I know she would like them if they suddenly appeared, which has happened when I let my guard down and allow her to indulge. But Finley's ability to move from simply dreaming of steaks to making that particular *there* a reality is a bit out of her reach.

So how did Bill Gates do it? And how can you bring your own desired future into reality? That is the subject of this chapter: the importance of vision and how it works to empower and sustain the process of realizing the *there* that you desire.

What Do You Want and Why?

Having been in the personal and leadership growth business for decades now, the term *vision* seems almost hackneyed. It's overused so much that sometimes it has even lost its meaning and its power. We all know what it is and speak of it frequently. "What's your vision?" we might ask. And then we assume that the answer given is truly one that matters, or more to our point, is going to mean something is really going to happen. Sometimes that's true, but sometimes not.

What is it, really, and when and how does it matter? What are vision's components? What kinds are most likely to succeed? Does it actually have power, and if so, where does that come from?

I remember a small company asking me to help them resolve significant dysfunction among the executive team, which was creating division, emotional upheaval, and lagging performance. In my work, I always say I get called in one of three scenarios: first, people or businesses that are doing well and want to always get better; second, people or businesses that are experiencing a known issue or problem they want to resolve; and third, people or businesses that are a real mess and about to blow up or disintegrate. This particular one was in the third category. I always want to have at least one of these hairballs in my case load, but not too many. They are painful, difficult, and tiresome. But I really learn a lot, and when we're successful, it is really rewarding. So, since I liked one of the principal executives in this particular one, I said, "Yes, I'll try to help."

I began by interviewing the three partners and the other two members of the executive team. I was surprised that, after all the dysfunction I had heard about, they were actually all likable people. When they told me about the culture of the team and the amount of conflict they were having and the ugliness they were living through, I was a bit surprised at what a good bunch of individuals they were. They seemed too nice and normal for that level of craziness and painful interactions. I was intrigued by how they were causing one another to regress into such childish behavior and by the lack of progress they were experiencing. I won't go into the entire case study, but will let you in on the most relevant point here. After the interviews, we all got together for an off-site at a retreat center. As they began to unload a bunch of conflicts and problems, I asked a question: "What do you guys want to build here? What is your vision for this company?"

They all looked at the founder, and he answered for everyone: "We want to be an X-dollar company." (I won't give you the amount because the same problem would exist if it were 10 million, 100 million, or hundreds of billions.) Immediately, my heart sank. They really didn't have to say any more than that for us to get to a starting point. I silently thought, "That might be the single worst 'vision' statement I have ever heard."

There is nothing wrong with revenue goals or other quantitative ways of measuring some aspects of success. We need those kinds of metrics for several reasons. But a revenue number is not a real vision, and it cannot do what we need a vision to do. Another company I recently talked with had a vision to "be the best company in the world" in their industry. It doesn't matter what the industry is; so what if you are the best paper clip company, car company, or whatever? This doesn't matter for several reasons. What if the second-best sucks? You have reached your vision as the best, but what does that make you? A little less sucky? What is the "best" anyway? What if you made it to your X-dollar revenue "vision"? What does it make you? What will you actually be doing? What will you be like? Will you like it? Who will you be helping? And how do these two "visions" help you learn how to get *there* in any specific way?

It's these kinds of specifics that the human body knows best.

When the brain comes up with a vision, it immediately possesses a lot more than the guy whose vision is "taking more or fewer steps to get across the room than anyone else." Instead, the brain desires to be in a great place to connect with everyone in the audience and communicate the message well. The brain has a vision that gives it *specificity* for its identity, mission, and something much more: the beginnings of the necessary elements to make it happen. Let's look at what a real vision contains, and what it accomplishes. Because as soon as you have one, the brain goes to work to attain it. Specificity does wonders for performance.

Desire First

We have called the vision a "desired future state." Let's start by looking at what *desire* does for us. Real desire has a specific object to satisfy it, and it originates from a specific need, hunger, or want. These needs or wants can originate from either positive desires or negative beginning states like pain, but both are powerful.

On the positive side, take Gates's vision as an example. A computer on every desk would enhance life and work in a myriad of *positive* ways, as illustrated by my writing this sentence on a portable computer in a much more desirable place than some computer lab. (I am actually in a very nice vineyard villa in Italy ☺.) Not to mention a million other applications a computer gives us that we are currently privileged to enjoy. That is a *positive* objective desire.

When I refer to needs generated from some negative reality, I mean a problem or pain to be solved. Martin Luther King Jr.

had a vision for a time when racism no longer ruled the day; his vision was to end something horribly negative. And, in that way, he also envisioned a positive outcome, but there was a specific horrible negative state he desired to end.

Let me reiterate a previous point: The path we are learning is applicable not only to worldwide technological shifts or nation-altering humanitarian goals; it applies to everything. The path is just the way that *anything* gets done. Fill the earth with computers, lose twenty pounds to lower blood pressure, or find an umbrella when it is raining. It all begins with a desire to get to something better or end something painful by achieving a specific objective outcome that describes *what will be different for whom.*

When your brain does come up with the vision, the real magic begins. Here are a few things that happen:

- When your desire is clear and specific, it begins to reign in your awareness of things relevant to your vision. You notice patterns, resources, people, opportunities, information, and so on that will all be needed to make the vision come to fruition. Your brain automatically engages a filter or a narrowed "search" of the world around you to help you get what you need to reach your vision. Think of it as a practical and useful bias of sorts, drawing on the brain's executive attention network that tunes you in to the activities and resources crucial to your vision. Your brain is doing real-time research and planning for you *just because you have a clear desire.* Neurologically, this happens in the reticular activating system as it gets primed to notice anything relevant to your goal. All this originated from *desire.* Have you ever noticed, for example, that as soon as you desire a new car, you begin to notice certain cars as you drive around each day? Or as soon as you desire to work out and get healthy, you start to notice how many other people are out walking and hitting the gym, too?

- Desire begins to morph into *motivation*, derived from electrical and chemical mechanisms in neurons and transmitters like dopamine. In other words, it gets you moving, even in small ways. This begins a chain reaction of activities that affect belief and behavior that, in turn, affect outcomes. This is fueled by the dopamine system and activity in the nucleus accumbens that creates anticipation. Motivation and the beginning of forward movement towards realizing a goal is underway, *as soon as you have the vision.* Direction is being set along with the anticipation of getting there. Energy is put into efforts to reach that future state.

- Because of all these complex brain functions, the hippocampus, which has to do with memory, begins to get called into action. Your brain is calling forth memories, experiences, and lots of data that will be needed for you to continue the path towards the realization of your vision. The wealth of neural connections from past experiences, both positive and negative, are all awakened to contribute to your desire.

- Most crucially, the prefrontal cortex gets called into duty for a host of activities that will make the vision become reality, such as planning, making decisions, impulse control, release of energy, and so on. Each part of the brain recruits other parts to come to the party. They are getting ready—all this because you are putting forth a vision. The "whole company" is beginning to get aligned.

I could go on about the neuroscience of desire and vision, but for our purposes, just remember this: A desired and clear vision is the very first step on your path to a desired future.

In addition to being specific, the desire must be *compelling* enough to get you and others moving, to get everyone on board. Are you hungry enough to get out of bed and make that sandwich? Sometimes yes, sometimes no, but the amount of hunger you feel is going to determine whether you actually get up and head to the kitchen or just roll over and go back to sleep. The same could be said for more life-altering visions, such as ushering in civil rights in America. The vision must be compelling enough to move armies, or even small groups, of people and networks to join in.

So, ask yourself: Do you want it—whatever *it* may be—enough to do more than just think about it? Do you want it enough to compel others to help you achieve it?

Many times, the little things you "forgot to do," like stop and pick up the dry cleaning, probably got forgotten because the desire wasn't strong enough to get the "whole company" aligned. There was no compelling vision. But if your boss had called to tell you that you were about to get an award in front of an audience of peers, you probably wouldn't forget to pick up that clean shirt. Desire matters.

Don't Forget Clarity

It is one thing to *want* something, to have a vision. Take AT&T in the year 1907. What if they only had a vision of building a phone company or helping people talk to each other? Would they have become what they ultimately were able to become? Probably not. But what Theodore Vail, the pioneering leader of the company that became AT&T, came up with as the vision was

"One Policy, One System, Universal Service." That kind of clarity shaped the company's trajectory and led them to where they are today, when their current vision is to "connect people with their world, everywhere they live and work. . . ." It drove activity and focus, prioritized resources, and much more—even laying down intercontinental underground connections spanning the ocean floor. Talk about vision driving specific activities.

When Martin Luther King Jr. said that a person should be judged by the content of his character and not the color of his skin, he expressed an idea that was very clear, specific, and objective. It organizes and focuses, and offers a compelling desire that people would activate around. It tapped into a great deal of pain and proposed a specific and objective ending to the pain, as well as an ending that would hold positive rewards.

A clear vision or goal gets all the brain's and body's resources moving in the ways that things happen. Even long before neuroscience could explain why specific visions and goals worked, this belief was found in popular collective wisdom. As Zig Ziglar used to say, "If you aim at nothing, you will hit it every time." Or as Alice in *Alice in Wonderland* says when she encounters the Cheshire Cat at the fork in the road:

Alice: Would you tell me, please, which way I ought to go from here?
The Cheshire Cat: That depends a good deal on where you want to get to.
Alice: I don't much care where.
The Cheshire Cat: Then it doesn't much matter which way you go.

Alice: . . . So long as I get somewhere.

The Cheshire Cat: Oh, you're sure to do that, if only you
    walk long enough.

Ouch. Two big elements are clear here in their conversation: *Knowing* where you want to get and *caring* where you get. That is what we are talking about. Clarity and desire. And as much research has demonstrated, clear, specific visions or goals are more likely to come to fruition than those that lack those characteristics. In the popular goal model called SMART goals, the first letter, S, stands for *specific*. To get organized, desire needs an object, a target. "I want a relationship" is not as compelling as "I want *you*." Or even as compelling as "I want a specific kind of relationship. A person with these qualities." Ask any woman if she is interested in a man who just wants *anyone*, or ask a man if he wants to sign up for a woman who is just interested in finding a husband. No, thank you. Specific desire is magic.

But It Takes More

It would be nice if a clear and motivating vision were enough, but science and experience tell us it is not, at least not on its own. It is necessary for sure, just not sufficient.

We saw how desire creates motivation and gets things moving. But there is a problem with what we subjectively experience as "motivation." It wanes. It varies. It is not consistent. But it is essential. And, on its own, it is not sufficient. As research on goal setting shows, several other elements equip us to make progress towards our goal even after motivation wanes. Let's look at those.

One of them we shall get to more deeply later, in Chapter 6, but I will mention it here because it starts with vision. That factor, the most important factor in reaching a goal, is *consistent action that moves things forward.* Just setting a clear and motivating vision triggers *the neurological functions that will lead to the consistent activities needed to support it.* These functions are first called into action as soon as the vision is created. In other words, the vision lays the groundwork for the consistent action you'll need later, even when you don't feel like doing it. The path is being formed already.

When the vision is clear, and desire is coupled with it, the brain calls into action other functions that begin planning and will be needed in decision making and self- control. This happens in the prefrontal cortex, as desire heats it up. It makes you *more* poised to delay gratification, which will help you keep going even when you don't feel like it, get distracted, or hit obstacles. In addition, as soon as any desire is acted upon, your brain activates reward loops that will reinforce your doing specific routines that support your goal.

Desire itself, although subjective and waning, activates neurocognitive brain functions that can get you moving in a direction and keep you going. Said another way, the vision begins to send the train down the track, and even helps lay down the track itself.

Now for the next element that needs to be coupled with your vision besides clarity and desire: belief.

The Power of Belief

You have seen it on a thousand cheesy motivational placards: "If you believe it, you can achieve it." Or as Henry Ford said, and I absolutely love this one, "The man who thinks he can and the man who thinks he can't are both right." Or as Napoleon Hill taught everyone, "Whatever the mind can conceive and believe, it can achieve." Always a Zig fan, I love his version, "Your attitude, not your aptitude, will determine your altitude."

When I was engaged to my wife, Tori, she wanted to go skydiving together for her birthday. I had zero desire for that vision, but I did have a desire to not wimp out on my fiancée's birthday. That vision got me to consider jumping out of a plane, but I *still* needed the belief that I could fly with the help of a parachute and some training from professionals. So, I had to get enough belief to actually do it.

You experience this every day. When you get out of a chair to walk from here to there, wherever *there* might be, you really *believe* you can do it. Your desire to get across the room, along with your belief that you can do it, makes it all work.

The same applies to situations you might be confronting for the first time:

- Starting a new career
- Making a never-before-hit financial goal
- Losing an amount of weight that seems impossible
- Getting "undepressed"
- Finding and having a successful relationship, or turning a failing one around
- Learning a new skill

You might have some other deep desire in business or life. And yet, in the deepest parts of your soul, you might doubt whether it is possible for you to realize these visions.

Without a belief that your vision is possible, things break down. The processes we have been discussing waver and sometimes even cease. For example, there is a condition called learned helplessness that has been documented for decades, where circumstances outside of your control lead you to doubt your ability to create an outcome. You don't really believe you can do anything to make it happen. It leads to depression and negative feelings about oneself and the future. And the result is—nothing happens. *Even when the desire is great.* In fact, the desire can make it worse; you want something so badly, but it seems out of reach for you, your team, or your business. That leads to depression and loss of energy. As the proverb says: "Hope deferred makes the heart sick." (Prov. 13:12)

Certainly, goals must be realistic. I am not going to ever win the Masters. Not at my age and ability. Nor am I going to play for the Lakers. "If I can believe it, I can achieve it" is just not true. In fact, if I believed that I could play professional basketball, someone who loves me should stop me from investing a lot of time, energy, or money in trying to play in the NBA. No matter what the law of attraction says, my visualizing myself defeating LeBron won't help.

But, as I often say to people, the "believing it is possible" factor should already be answered for what most of us think of doing. Take the list above: launching careers, making money, losing weight, getting over depression, or finding a relationship. People do *all of those things each and every day*—people who are probably like you, demographically and otherwise. So, you can check off the "belief" box in this way: You can absolutely believe that it can be done because it is already being done. A lot of testimonies and stories from other people should tell you that.

I have been mentoring a young man who wants to own a business, but got stuck and was giving up. When I asked him why, he said, "Businesses cost money, and I don't have any yet. It will be a long time before I have enough money to begin." That was his belief: that it was impossible to do without money was rendering his vision dead in the water.

I literally laughed out loud. "That is ridiculous," I said. "In fact, many, if not most, businesses are not started with the visionary's money. It is usually someone else's money. It's called an investor, or a partner, or a funding source."

"Seriously?" he asked. "They start or buy a business with no money?"

I had already figured out that trying to convince him that it was possible would be less powerful than offering examples and testimonies that proved my point. So, I began with one: Starbucks. I said, "Did you know that Howard Schultz had a vision and no money when he launched Starbucks? He wanted to buy a small coffee company and turn it into his ultimate vision. So, he raised money from some local people, including Bill Gates's father. If he were thinking like you, he would still be an employee at a little company, and you would not know what a Starbucks was because it would not exist."

My point is that most of what we dream is actually being done in the real world. That young man's belief was wrong. The good news is we can use reality to draw us away from our fears or limiting beliefs.

But—and this is critical—you really, really need to believe it.

I am not asking you to believe that you can fly without a parachute or play in the NBA at my age and height or with my lack of talent. I am just asking you to believe that what is being done every day by someone like you, is possible to accomplish! That is all. That is why we have people share their testimonies.

The power of that belief reinforces your desire. "I think I can" gets the little train up the hill (because trains have made it up hills before). When people begin to see that something is possible, it changes everything. Again, that's why testimonies from those who have done it (and you can too!) are so helpful. One of my favorite examples happens on Dave Ramsey's show when people visit the studio and do the Debt-Free Scream. People fly into Ramsey's Nashville studio from all over the country, having gotten themselves out of sometimes hundreds of thousands of dollars of debt with little income, using his methods. They get to go on the air and scream "I am DEBT FREE!!!!" As they do that, others in the listening audience of millions are getting a vision of how to get out of their own pile of debt, but more than that, they are getting, in real time and real life, the belief that it is possible. Dave Ramsey's own story of the steps he took in his twenties to go from bankruptcy to being wealthy is not only inspiring, but also gives others the you-can-too belief.

Until desire is coupled with the belief that something is possible, we will probably be stuck. But when belief begins to grow, worlds can change. Consider the kids that an organization called First Star works with in Los Angeles. They focus on kids in the foster care system, a population with about a 50 percent high school graduation rate and a college-enrollment rate of only 10 percent. But kids who engage in First Star's program have a very different outcome. *Check out these numbers: 98 percent of their foster care kids graduate from high school, and nearly 90 percent enroll in higher education.* Having been personally involved with their work, I could go on and on about their methods and why they work. But for our purposes here, research reports this incredible finding: 94 percent of their students say what changes their lives is *"believing that college is possible for them."* First Star not only gave them the vision, but joined desire with belief, helping the kids see what was possible for them.

Several elements go into First Star's approach, but one is that their trainings and weekend and summer experiences take place on a college campus. I have spent time with them at UCLA, and witnessed foster care kids seeing a university for the first time, *experiencing* being there, *finding* they can feel comfortable there, *learning* the path and the steps to get there, *learning* that money could be found, and so forth. All these factors go into believing it is possible for them.

It's no surprise that research shows that optimists have better outcomes in various areas than pessimists: they believe it can be done. Desire *plus* belief gets the human body moving. Belief activates something psychologists and neuroscientists call agency, which means you realize that you have control of the area of your life that you want to change, and you have control of the levers to get you there.

So next time you ask yourself "Is this possible?" look for examples and real-world testimonials to check yourself. Put that newfound or renewed belief together with a clear, compelling, and specific vision, and you will be able to say "I can, too." You can pass on that same optimism to others on your team as well.

It's not a one-time effort. You must consistently remind yourself and others of what's possible and why.

But I Can't Wait Forever

We all know people with dreams that remain only dreams. Even worse, we probably know those who have done a little work on their dreams, which remain unrealized. While there are many reasons for this, one of them is that there is no deadline associated with the vision. When JFK said we would reach the moon "before this decade is out," the dream became a vision, in large part because he created urgency and a timeline for its achievement. Why did this matter? Because our brains love timelines. According to research, goals are more likely to be fulfilled when they come with an achieve-by date. Setting a date creates a sense of urgency, which helps to allocate your attention and planning more effectively, and awakens monitoring processes internally and organizationally.

It is why, when your vision is to give your presentation from the other side of the room *right now,* you tend not to lollygag or get lost along the way. "Gotta get moving," the brain says to your entire body, activating a planning process to make its moves, something we will turn to in Chapter 6.

So, as you work on your vision, keep a realistic timeline in mind for getting there. Ask, "How will we know when we have achieved it?" It will be like the weather service telling you when sunrise will occur tomorrow, in that there will be a moment when you will be able to say, "It is daylight." And, along the way, you will begin to feel it getting a little brighter each moment. It may be a specific date or time, but it also might be an ongoing sequence of events to mark your progress. Either way, it is important that you have a sense of "by when" associated with what you want to bring into reality.

This adds clarity and removes vagueness. Another thing the brain loves? Clarity.

What About You?

In Chapter 1, I said that we all have an issue in that we tend to just get to it and begin to work on getting *there* without looking at *how* we are doing it. Often, we don't have a good map to work with *and* we tend to "go to it" in our own way. We do things the way we are already wired to do them. We create and build businesses, departments, and even our own pursuits "in our own image." They begin to look a lot like us. While that is great in many ways, we all have gaps between who we are and what is needed to get *there*.

We have all seen great visionaries who begin companies but lack the ability to execute or the desire to do the detailed work that execution requires. And until they find a person great in operations to join them, their efforts are scattered, and results may remain lackluster. We have also seen great "managers" who lack big visions and tend to deliver more of the same, only slightly improved. The entity never becomes what it could be because it was held back by the manager's weaknesses or tendency to work "in their own image."

Some of this is not going to change in an individual, as they are not wired for a particular function. We all know people who are excellent in execution but will never be visionaries, and vice versa. We all know great encouragers of talent who are great "people people" but aren't at all strategic in how they think. That is not bad, nor does it mean someone is not a valuable team member. It just means, as the Strengths Movement has emphasized, that none of us has all the talents needed to accomplish what we desire. We need others, as we shall see in Chapter 4, which is on talent.

While we may lack some strengths, we have opportunities for personal growth that we can, and sometimes must, do in every area. For example, I lived in LA for a long time. I was often asked by people from around the country who visited my office in Beverly Hills, "Do you know any actors?"

I would always say, "Yes, want to meet some today?"

Surprised, they would say, "Sure! How?"

"Let's go to lunch," I would tell them. "There will be some there."

Before they got too excited, I would explain that at pretty much every restaurant we could go to, they would meet an actor. And the actor would be the server waiting on our table. The restaurant world in LA is filled with them, for good reason. Anyone just beginning in their acting career must pay the rent, and many work in restaurants while they are trying to build a résumé and get a break. It's totally normal, and in fact, admirable in my view. Working hard until you make it is a key to success.

But I also have had many experiences where I asked my server to tell me about themselves, where they were from, and so on, and they would say, "I moved here from the Midwest to work on my acting [or screenwriting] career. I am an actor [or screenwriter]," and I would ask, "Wonderful! So, have I seen something you are in [or have written]?"

And then they would say something that would begin to sound flimsy and vague, like, "I am working on a script right now about . . ." Or "I have a good connection who might get me an audition for a new series . . ." but nothing really tangible. There's no *there* yet, to speak of. This is not unusual for people just starting out. They haven't had enough time to get really rolling.

I would usually respond, "Sounds great! Hope it works out!" and then I would ask them, "So how long have you been here doing that?"

Many times, the response would be, "Not that long, a couple of years or so." But many more times, the answer would be "for years" and sometimes "decades." And yet nothing has happened.

I would bet that most of the waiters/actors I have met, including those who have been stalled for decades, are very talented actors or writers. I would bet that talent is not the problem; otherwise, they wouldn't be here. Acting or writing was probably their strength for sure. But an aspiring actor who doesn't have enough ability in their non-strength areas to prevent their personal weaknesses from derailing them will never get there. If they can't discipline themselves enough to learn lines, make connections, have a plan and strategy to get auditions, secure agents, show up on time, rewrite scripts, and so on—it's just not going to happen for them. At some point, where we have weaknesses, we must address those gaps and make sure they do not derail us. We must address how our gaps may be keeping us from *there*.

So with that, let's look at some areas of personal growth that apply to vision.

INTERNAL LIMITS

Having a BHAG (a big hairy audacious goal), a term coined by Jim Collins and Jerry Porras in *Built to Last,* pushes us to greater achievements, is emotionally compelling, and provides a lot of focus and a rallying cry that aligns people to get there. It stretches us to more growth.

But what if you come from a background like the foster kids I mentioned, an environment with lots of internal limits to how big your vision can be based on your past experience?

What if you have internal voices from your childhood and young adulthood that say, "Who do you think you are? You could never do that!" What if you have heard the voice of failure saying, "That is really difficult, and I [we] might fail." Your internal voice is stifling your dreams and desires.

Google cofounder Larry Page's internal limits were forever changed when he was a student and attended a leadership institute at the University of Michigan. There, he was taught to "have a healthy disregard for the impossible." So what happened when he shifted his internal thinking? He thought something like, "What if we saved every URL on the entire internet and downloaded them?" An immediate internal thought might have been: "That's impossible! We don't have enough RAM." But he had changed that internal limit to not hold him back, and now we have Google.

When you get rid of internal limits, you don't know what can happen. But more to the point, getting rid of internal limits affects what kind of vision you can even come up with! What voices or beliefs in you, or your team, or your board, are keeping your vision too small?

If your team asks, "How can we build a company to help

people get across town?" You might open a new taxi service or a scooter rental. But if you ask, "How can I get a perfect stranger to pick me up any time of day, anywhere I am, in their own car, and take me anywhere I want to go, and have no money change hands?" Then, you come up with Uber. You might be thinking too small, unable to craft a bigger vision.

But sometimes the opposite is true. Some people are thinking too big for where they are and have grandiose dreams, when a smaller one might fit better.

Visions and goals have to be realistic. Google and Uber were realistic, as we now know. But a thirteen-year-old who just got his first computer and says "I am going to create a technology company today" might want to right-size his vision, at least for a while.

Our visions should never be limited, but they must take into account reality.

You don't have to let uninformed or inexperienced naysayers diminish you, but you do need to get feedback from the right sources—from people who have experience doing something somewhat related to what you're trying to do and from people who know you and may see weaknesses—and strengths—you can't see yourself. Make sure your feet are firmly planted in reality. This is one way to assess whether your thinking is too limiting or too grand, at least for right now.

TOO SMALL

Just as the foster kids in the First Star program had not been exposed to a bigger way of thinking, and as my clinical experience had not exposed me to creating a scalable healthcare company, your world might not be large enough either. You may never have seen what is being done in the area that you want to build, or even in other industries that might apply to yours.

Many CEOs and teams that I work with spend a lot of time going to competitors' stores, websites, and social media platforms to see how the world may be bigger than they know. I recently took a very seasoned leader to the Global Leadership Summit in Chicago to listen to speakers talk about what they had done and how they had done it, and he said that his world was greatly enlarged. His vision had increased and had been energized. And he has a lot of experience and success already.

Reading about others, going to conferences, visiting businesses, networking—all these and other activities expand one's world and begin to show what is possible, what can be done that they never dreamed of. Even when it comes to a personal growth challenge such as addiction, a first-timer's experience at a recovery meeting allows them to hear personal accounts from formerly hopeless addicts who have now been sober for a long time. Hearing how others did it enlarges the world of possibility. We all need to see *more* and to hear *more* to know *more* is possible for us, too.

TOO MANY VOICES

We need to get realistic feedback to fine-tune a vision. But, we do *not* need critical people clouding our thinking about what is possible—and all too often, what they think is not possible. We know from research that the people you surround yourself with are the biggest determinant of how you'll end up, whether it's health or wealth.

I'm not saying I don't love my dysfunctional and curmudgeonly friends. A few of them are my favorites! It is like having Eeyore alongside to add comedy to every situation, as they express negative, self-deprecating humor. But, they are not the friends that I engage when thinking about goals or next steps, especially for feedback or advice, as I know their outlook will be pessimistic and produce a list of a hundred ways to explain why it won't work. Even if it is about "I could never do that," their own lack of self-belief is limiting and contagious. I want to be around people who think things are possible, and people who do the impossible.

You might have to look at the voices that surround you, personally and professionally. If there is a preponderance of fear or pessimism, or a lack of an abundance mentality, then you *must* inoculate yourself against those voices. Get a vaccine to protect you from pessimism and small-world voices. That might mean someone is not right for your team, or it might mean that you just need to be careful who you include in your vision. You do *not* need negativity. Informed feedback from optimists, yes, but not feedback that will douse your fire. Don't share or create your vision in a cesspool of negativity and limited thinkers.

Other Internal Areas to Examine

- When you dream of a vision, do you fear failure or rejection? What are you doing to address these fears?
- When you need to cast a vision to your team or investors or anyone else, does a little voice say, "But why would they believe me? Or follow me? Or invest in me?"

- When you think of your vision and what it will take to get there, do you only see limitations of resources? Or talent? Or circumstances?
- When you dream of a new vision or goal, do you immediately see your past failures telling you what you can expect if you try again?
- Are there any other limiting or negative thoughts or voices that you see? How will you address these?

The internal reasons for limiting or not pursuing a vision are endless. That is why so many people are dreamers and not visionaries. They have fantasies, but not visions. A vision is a desired future state, and *state* means it *will* exist. Listen for the noise in your head, or even in your team, that is either limiting your vision or throwing cold water on it before it can even catch fire. Remember, if someone is doing it, it can be done. And there are visions that no one is already doing that one day will get done, too, if you can only believe. At one point, no one was doing Amazon!

Moving On

Here we are with your having seen the first of the big five essentials that will get you to your desired future: vision. We have seen how the human body approaches it and why all those components are essential to the process. As you examine them and put them in place, the odds of your desired future becoming a reality increase drastically. Seeing is believing, and believing leads to doing.

Also, we have examined how, even if vision is not your primary strength, it does not have to hold you back. You just need to en-sure that someone has it, in the ways described in this chapter, and then execute.

Even if vision is not your strength, it will be key to look at these growth steps. For you to properly align with a great vision, the personal growth steps will be important in preventing it from becoming impaired, even if the talent you bring on creates the vision or helps you to do so. Those steps will help you not diminish it or limit it. I want you to have full throttles behind what you envision accomplishing.

Now, having seen the importance of vision, it is time to begin taking the steps essential to making it a reality. The next step is engaging the talent. Let's go there now.

CHAPTER 4

Engaging Talent:
We Go Nowhere Alone

We have seen that the first step in the path from here to there is to create the vision for what a desired future would be—its *there*. Martin Luther King Jr. saw a day when skin color didn't matter. Bill Gates saw computers everywhere, on every desk. You can certainly think of other great visions, but they all have one thing in common: The *thought*, the *picture* in the brain of that desired future, does not suddenly turn into a reality because the brain dreams it up. Nothing changes at all in the outside world with just a thought or a mental picture. It has to be built into something tangible.

Fair enough, brain. Nothing comes without effort, so get to it. Go change the world. *Go, brain, go. Get moving . . . Come on, brain . . . hop to it.*

And then . . . nothing! Why am I still standing *here*, not *there*? Here is the news flash: A brain goes nowhere by itself.

Fortunately, your brain knows that. So, it takes the next step of engaging *the talent it needs to get there.* In a fraction of a second, it has asked a question: What talents (abilities, roles, players) are required to get me to the other side of the room? And after figuring that out, it goes to work recruiting its team. It figures, "I am going to need a couple of legs, some eyes to see where I am going, inner ears to balance me, lungs to suck down some extra O_2 . . ."

All this happens so quickly that you are not even aware of it. Your brain begins sending the impulses out, the recruiting calls, to the talent that is going to be needed: recruiting, motivating, aligning, onboarding with instructions.

The CEO, the prefrontal cortex, has already come up with the vision and weighed the critical factors, such as strength of desire, potential rewards, possibility of achievement, and the like, as we discussed in Chapter 3. But now, it is activating systems to help plan movement, integrate visual and spatial information through the posterior parietal cortex, and signal other systems that will be involved in distance, direction, and even our posture as we make our move across the room. Other systems, like the basal ganglia and cerebellum, will later help to increase efficiency and suppress competing motor actions that might interfere.

The primary motor cortex sends out commands to wake up and activate the players, through the spinal cord, coordinating upper and lower motor neurons that recruit the skeletal muscles to do the heavy lifting. And don't forget the other positions that will be needed—sensory help to see where it is going, and maintain balance, while addressing the energy demands that will be answered with an increased heart rate to generate oxygen for our breath.

Without these players, all coming together in a coordinated

fashion, this vision is just a thought or a fantasy, going nowhere and floundering with frustration. Just one more dreamer, still waiting tables decades later.

So, what does that have to do with becoming a singer-songwriter and producing music? Or winning a Super Bowl? Or building an aerospace company that does a lot of what NASA used to do?

No One Does It Alone

Our youngest daughter, Lucy, has always been an artist, ever since she was a tiny person. As a young child, she went through the days singing. And once she was old enough to write, she started carrying a little book around with her, jotting down her thoughts, rhymes, and such. A corollary, seen often with that kind of talent, is that she is also not the most structured or linear person. She would naturally be very good at being either *here* or *there*, but defining an organized way to get from one to the other would not be on her natural radar. She is the living definition of "in the moment," although she has always been a busy work-horse, doing art and cooking projects. So, she's neither lazy nor non-productive. She accomplishes a lot, just not in a very systematic way (at least it seems that way to others). She's not a huge planner. I love her for it, and her artistic nature has always made me smile. But both sides of her artistic makeup brought us to this moment: One day in her mid-teen years, I was in the kitchen, and she walked in and said, "Dad . . . I have a question. How do people become singer-songwriters? That is what I want to do."

"Really?" I said. Although not surprised, I had never heard her state it in such a definitive way.

"Well . . . let me help you," I said. Immediately, I left the kitchen, got my big whiteboard, and wheeled it in. She rolled her eyes, thinking, "Here comes another psychologist-dad life lesson," like she and her sister had made fun of while growing up imprisoned in my classroom.

"So, Luce . . . there really is kind of a GPS map you can use to think about this. A map that can help you get where you want to go. I want to share it with you," I started. By now, you might have guessed what was coming.

I put a big #1 up on the left side and under it wrote the word "Vision."

"Luce . . . tell me your vision . . . what is it you want to do? Want to be? What would it look like?" And I was amazed. This obviously was not the first time she'd given some thought to where she wanted to go. She painted a clear and cogent picture of what a career in music would look like. I was impressed. She could even name a few specific artists who embodied all that she wanted to do and why.

"Great," I said. "That is really impressive that you have thought it out that much and know so clearly what you want. You are way ahead of the game. So now, let's go to number two."

Next, I wrote "#2–Engage Talent." And then I said, "After knowing your vision, you have to figure out what talent you are going to need to get you there."

She immediately looked up and said quizzically, "But wait . . . you and Mom said I have talent . . . right?"

"Of course you have talent, Luce. But I am not talking about *your* talent. *I am talking about the other talent you are going to need to help you reach your vision.* Who is going to be on your team to help you get there? Who is going to help? What talent do you need around you besides you?" I clarified.

Immediately she got it. "*Oh . . .*" she said. "Well, first thing I need is a new guitar teacher."

"Why's that?" I asked. I knew the guy, and he seemed nice.

"I just feel like I have been stuck for a while, and I find myself going on YouTube to learn some new chords and things that he doesn't really teach me. We just keep doing the same old stuff," she explained.

"Okay . . . great. We can do that. What else?"

"Well, I need to start performing more. I don't know where or how, but I need some way to get some auditions and begin singing more in front of people. I don't know where to find those," she said. She had done a few school plays but not much else. We talked about some people Tori and I knew and other options, and then she continued into topics like studio production and how she knew nothing about how to do that, and other issues that she would need help with. Management, production, getting on the streaming platforms, and so forth.

I won't go through our working out the whole structure of the path we are talking about in this book but wanted to mention it here as it relates to her one illustrative comment back to me when I mentioned engaging talent. Her reply was classic: "You and Mom said I have talent." *She thought I meant her*, and it didn't occur to her that realizing her vision did not just depend on how good she was at singing or songwriting. It was going to also depend on another factor she had never thought about: Who do I need to help me get there?

(And she followed through on that question. She was able to

join up with an award-winning producer. Also, when Kevin Jonas Sr., the former pastor who championed his three sons' musical career as the Jonas Brothers, heard her sing, he said he wanted to help as well. Long story short, her song "Crash and Learn" was bought by CBS and the CW television networks for placement in two network television shows, with her song featured on all the big platforms. She has continued to perform and write music. As a young artist, she has found momentum. She just released a new EP called *Allowing Time*. I am proud of her.)

But for our purposes, it brings up a key point. No one does it alone. The brain can't move without the body, no matter how smart the brain is. And yet we often forget this or don't give it the attention and weight it deserves.

Let's Win . . . But How?

Imagine being the holder of six Super Bowl rings and getting a call to come join a team with a losing 7–9 record that had not even qualified for the playoffs for twelve consecutive seasons. *Um* . . . likely to pass. Unless you were Tom Brady.

The story is worth exploring in detail, but for our purposes here, one point stands out. When Brady was looking at this opportunity, he evaluated the *here* (a team that can't even make the playoffs) and looked at the *there* (winning another Super Bowl with this team) and realized something: It is possible, but *not with the talent that is there now*. Let me repeat: He did *exactly* what the human brain does when looking at how to get from here to there for the vision. He asked the crucial second question, "What talent do I need to engage to get there?" He found it lacking.

Upon scanning the scenario, he next did exactly what the brain does and engaged exactly the talent needed. First, he figured out what positions (the particular skills) would be needed, and then he recruited the specific people. Jim Collins famously referred to this as figuring out first the seats needed on the bus and then which individuals would sit in those seats. Brady decided on at least four positions and identified individuals, among other inputs: tight end Rob Gronkowski . . . wide receiver Antonio Brown . . . running back Leonard Fournette . . . and kicker Ryan Succop.

Suffice it to say, it worked! The team won the Super Bowl the next year.

Both Brady and Lucy needed to get the talent in place to reach their desired futures. This stepping stone on the path doesn't just apply to football players and teenagers who want to write and release songs. It's also a crucial step for someone with a vision for space travel.

When Elon Musk had a vision for SpaceX, he was not an aerospace engineer. But his vision was clear and specific: Make humans a multiplanetary species. And what did he do next after obsessively studying the field and determining what was needed? He recruited the talent needed to build the company he had envisioned, including propulsion expert Tom Mueller and others. And don't forget this fact either: He was able to attract brilliant talent not because of money, but because of the *compelling vision*. In Jungian terms, he sought out the whole, the integration of the parts, to produce an effect larger than each one on its own.

I can't tell you how many times I have said to a CEO after learning about his or her team, "You are one *hire* away from success." It would be very clear that a key "seat on the bus," in Collins's words, a key position or key talent or skill that was necessary to get *there*, was either missing or insufficient. "Go hire one of those now!" I would find myself saying.

I learned this by accident years ago, when I had the vision for an integrated psychiatric hospital. At the time, inpatient psych was practiced in a way that I always felt was disintegrated. Psychiatrists and psychologists would admit patients, and the hospital unit would have a milieu somewhat separate from the experts doing the actual treatment (i.e., the doctors). It was disjointed and not all working together towards a sharp vision of healing. In addition, I wanted to make a hospital unit that was more faith welcoming than was typical at the time, when someone's faith was often seen as part of the problem, not part of the solution.

So, I set out and began. Early on, I asked Dr. John Townsend (talent) to join me and build out this vision together. And that is what we did. We built out the vision, but we did it, as I said earlier, *in our own image.* In other words, being doctors in private practice, we pretty much hired talent in the same way a private practice model would. We hired great doctors and some administrative staff. And we opened one hospital and were doing fine, really loving what we were getting to do and accomplishing. Until . . . a staff member invited a friend of his to join us for dinner one night after our call-in radio show. We had never met him, but he had just retired from being the chief operations officer (COO) of a big hospital chain. Early in the dinner, he asked us about our call center, including how it operated and where it was. John and I looked at each other and said, "What's a call center?" We had just always fielded inquiries like a private practice does. Someone calls and sets up an appointment.

We were suddenly awakened to knowing what we didn't know and a vast number of "unknown unknowns" about the industry we had launched into. Thinking we were going along well, we had no idea what the right talent could do for our vision. Our talent was treating patients. We were clinicians. We suddenly realized we needed healthcare operational talent we didn't possess or even knew existed. (Cut me some slack . . . I was in my late twenties when I started this company ☺.)

This led to our discovery of how larger healthcare chains are organized, the integration of marketing efforts to streamline paths into treatment, insurance authorization processes, managed care contracts, and so on. We were clinicians, so we had built a healthcare company with a clinician's mindset only, *in our own image.* That was also our strength and our strategy, as our treatment *always put the patient and their clinical needs before business.* That was our brand differentiation, what we were known for, but our limited know-how and private practice mindset were limiting the scope and scale of our vision.

That's when we asked our dinner companion, Bob Whiton, to come on board. He became our COO, his expertise and talent joining with ours to help us see that this vision we had was scalable. We could help many more people with what we had built. Long story short: In a couple of years, we had developed a company with hospital units and clinics in forty-five markets throughout the western United States. I learned something valuable, even though it was the hard way and probably meant we had wasted a few years: The right talent is everything. Or, to continue the analogy to the human body, the brain had found its legs.

I heard once that Peter Drucker was asked in a private meeting, "What is the most important thing a leader does?" He closed his eyes for about a minute and then said, "Defining WHO does WHAT." Bingo. It's getting the right talent in the right spots and, as we shall see in Chapter 6, doing the *what*, meaning the specific activities that will make a difference. But for now, the point is this: Find the *who* to do the *what*.

Not Just Business

While we have been looking at several business examples, remember that this five-part path doesn't just apply to business and leadership.

When I was in clinical practice, especially hospital practice, a common scenario would be an initial meeting with a patient who was depressed, had an anxiety disorder, or experienced some other issue. In that session, they would often report something to the effect of "I've tried everything, and nothing works." I would generally find that what they actually meant was that they had tried everything that *they knew* to do or everything that a well-meaning friend, pastor, or relative knew to do. They felt lost and hopeless, but in reality, they were just one step away from getting well. They just needed help from someone with the right knowledge and experience.

The path we are discussing applies to most all we do. If someone is going to get over a significant depression, for example, my experience and a lot of research will tell you that there are going to be multiple parties involved. When I was putting together treatment plans, I lobbied for a team comprised of a therapist providing individual therapy, a psychiatrist, group therapy of some kind, the involvement of a few close friends, a general physician, and a safe community to provide structure and routine. Building a team of talent is essential in other situations as well, besides business. For example, if someone is going to lose weight and has never been able to do that, to think that they are going to suddenly be able to do it without direction, knowledge, structure, support, and so on is wishful thinking. The same is true for personal finance, which is why out-of-control couples or individuals enlist help through something like a Financial Peace group to gain knowledge and a support system.

Whether it's a business challenge, a personal issue, or a financial crisis, we need to ask the question: Who do I need in this picture with me in order to get there? People who do this increase the likelihood of reaching their desired future.

Some of the talent might be professional, like a consultant, psychologist, special subject matter expert, personal trainer, coach, financial planner, business coach, or other professionals to join your team to get *there*. Others are not paid, like mentors, friends, coworkers, or even professional networks you join to get into the path of deal flow or opportunity windows. The point is that every endeavor to get *there* requires others. So ask yourself, early and often: *What talent do we need? Who do we need to bring in? Who do we need in the loop? What networks do we need to connect with?* And *never* forget your personal networks. You have many friends who know something, or at least know someone who does!

How Big Is Your Circle?

Sometimes we do not draw the circle large enough. I was doing an offsite with one of the largest HVAC companies in the United States for their service teams. These were the guys in the trucks who would go to a big box store in the middle of the summer when the AC had gone down. That is not a good moment. Their customers, the big box stores, are not happy and want cool air fast because none of *their* customers want to go into a Walmart, Target, or Home Depot in Texas in August when it is 100 degrees outside and no air-conditioning inside. Hot air means lost sales.

At the offsite, we started with the team's vision. It was interesting to see that they pretty much thought their vision for a service call was to fix something and get it working again. That sounded less than compelling to me, so we went to work. Here is where they finally landed: "At the end of the service call, we want _____ to tell us they are 'glad their AC broke down, so they got the opportunity to deal with and experience us.'" Now, *that* is a compelling *there* for HVAC service people.

As we massaged that vision and fleshed it out to consider what would have to happen for a customer to feel that way, it naturally led to the kind of service that would be required, and one element was speed and lack of disruption to the store and its managers. So, in line with what we are talking about in this chapter, the next question was: *What talent do we need to engage for that to happen?*

From that one question emerged two ambitious new practices that changed everything. One was a new process. When the call first came in, they began to immediately call into action the home office and get any remotely imaginable, hypothetical parts for that customer's equipment available and on the truck, before they even knew the problem. Second, and even more impactful, they began calling the *store* manager to engage their staff before the service call so everyone would be better prepared for when the technicians arrived on-site. That might entail making the loading dock accessible before they arrived or clearing aisles or shelving spaces. The service truck team no longer saw their task as just going out and working on something. They saw it as a *there* that was ultimately going to require them to involve others, and they began to engage that talent earlier and bring them together so that their new vision could come to fruition.

There are two things to notice. First, they had to get to a more compelling vision than just fixing an AC. But second, almost every vision or goal we can embark upon is going to involve concentric circles of people and talent, paid and unpaid, to be realized. To begin with the end in mind, *just as the human body does*, and reverse engineer, is crazy effective.

One more example. A home builder I worked with was looking at the profitability of development projects. The home builder was already doing the usual things to maximize profit, so where else could they look to find more profit? Speed. As long as the project was not yet fully built and sold out, the builder was carrying a lot of costs for construction loans, materials, and so forth. If he could build faster and sell properties more quickly, he'd find profitability sooner because those carrying costs would be reduced. So how could he get faster?

The company used subcontractors for all the various pieces: driveways, drywalling, electrical, plumbing, and so on. As he began to study projects, process questions emerged such as,

"Why didn't the drywall get done before that particular week?" Answer: "Well, we had to wait for the paving to happen first and set in order to get the trucks in" or something like that. So the builder had an idea.

He brought all the talent together, all the subcontractors who previously had no relationship with each other. They were all individually hired and reported to project managers. Instead, he began bringing them together before the project began so they could work on the sequencing. And answers began to emerge like, "Well, we could let you know when we are going to pour concrete, and you could come the day before and deliver the drywall *before* we pour. Then you wouldn't have to wait for it to dry to get your trucks in." Other solutions were found when the talent was engaged from the beginning. And it worked. Another move the builder made was to tell all the subcontractors that if they worked together to increase speed, he would share the savings from finishing faster with *all* of them.

Here's an interesting side note from neuroscience: The brain is constantly sending out *messages* and impulses through networks of billions of neurons. Think of these as short e-mails going out to all the players, telling them they are needed, and when to show up. That is the first step towards engagement—naming them and then recruiting them.

Secondly, it is not a one-time message. It is an ongoing communication and engagement process. And the kicker is that we now know that the brain is constantly learning and adapting through neuroplasticity and is engaging in predictive action as well. It begins to prepare and anticipate your movements and actions. (That might explain why NBA players and other athletes seem to be in position to grab the ball that no one else saw coming.) The brain knows how to engage its talent, which predicts what will be needed so the brain can adapt. Again, the integrated whole works best.

One Hard Truth

I wrote a book called *Necessary Endings*. The main point of the book is that to get to the future you desire, some things that exist *today* cannot continue to exist. Their season has passed for whatever reason. To continue as things are, without ending them, will keep you stuck where you are. Doing too many things or continuing to do things that are no longer needed dilutes focus and resources.

The most difficult endings usually involve people. In the context we are talking about here, it means that sometimes *the talent around you is not going to be the talent that you need to get to your vision.* That is what Tom Brady saw. Whereas a new venture can begin by recruiting new talent, sometimes you find yourself in a situation with people already on the bus. Maybe they were a good fit in the past or for some former vision. Possibly, you made a bad choice back then that you failed to deal with. Or, they could have drifted into nonperformance or a thousand other issues that make what they bring to the table less than what is going to get you there. Put simply, sometimes you'll need to part ways with some people for your *there* to be realized.

Of course, these are tough choices. For some people in their personal lives, that means that they have to say goodbye to some friends. That is a common scenario in the lives of addicts who want to get sober or for others who want to change their lives.

They realize that their circle of friends, their community, or even a mentor they've outgrown must change as well.

In businesses, sometimes it is a hard realization that someone in a particular position no longer fits the new vision or the demands of the current one because they have not grown into their new position or are not performing. Again, there are lots of different circumstances and dynamics involved that can bring one to this kind of moment, but it is important to realize that engaging the talent you need sometimes means replacing the talent you have. It's a tough realization, often painful, but sometimes there are necessary endings in life. (Take a look at *Necessary Endings* for more on these dynamics.)

Keep Them Engaged

When the brain recruits a leg to begin the walk across the room, to get to *there*, it is not a one-time signal. It continues to send impulses to motivate the leg and keep it engaged. In the deep regions of the spinal cord, central pattern generators called neural circuits produce rhythms of repetitive movements, which stimulate muscle fibers in the legs. Without ongoing messaging, forward progress would stop.

The body can teach us here. Many leaders might be good at bringing someone onboard, but once the honeymoon phase is over, they forget that continuous engagement is needed and they leave gaps between engaging moments. As a result, the other party, the talent that is needed, feels either ignored or, worse, disheartened.

Engaging talent means more than identifying and recruiting. It means staying connected, nourishing, motivating, empowering, and coaching. It means team meetings and one-on-ones held at the appropriate cadence, connecting with direct reports, investors, alliances, and customers. Don't let too many gaps in connection show up. The brain keeps the legs moving.

Create Psychological Safety

The brain knows if it is safe to take the next step or not. Many sensory networks are always exercising due diligence as to whether the next move is okay to make or not. In fact, the entire human body is wired physically, neurologically, psychologically, spiritually, and mentally to ask one question before anything else, continuously, 24/7: *Am I safe?* If it gets a green light, it moves forward. But a yellow light will tell it to slow down, and a red light to stop.

You have been breathing, I hope, carelessly as you read this. That is because your system has kept sensory data coming in to let you know the air is safe to breathe. But, if it got a whiff of a gas fume, your attention would be drawn to that smell and you would get a yellow light. If it were bad enough, you might run for the nearest exit. The human body will keep itself safe, internally and externally, above all else. If it ever does feel endangered, the fight, flight, or freeze defense system will kick in. Push back, pull away, or be frozen in fear, unable to act.

So, again, the body teaches us well. What it does for its arms and legs, you also have to be doing to keep your talent engaged. You must be asking 24/7: Is your talent feeling safe? Are your key stakeholders feeling safe with you? Safe to speak their minds, share what they see, disagree with you when they have a different opinion? Confront you when you need to be corrected? Challenge the status quo? Have you provided clarity around their roles, so they know what steps they are free to take and which ones are off-limits? Is there a clear understanding of what is required from them? Do they know what is considered success for them? Do they know what the norms of expected behavior are and what is out of bounds?

Just as the body must feel safe from harm to function at its peak, you and your people must, too. Much research has been done on psychological safety in organizations, in marriage, and in virtually every other human endeavor. The evidence is overwhelming. When people feel safe, they perform better, learn better, and are more efficient. Productivity improves up to 50 percent, with almost 80 percent more engagement, 74 percent less stress, 27 percent reduced turnover, and 57 percent higher collaboration, the data show. We will examine this further in Chapter 8.

For people to feel heard, valued, and empowered is huge. The body does that well, providing health, safety, and support to the talent, as well as continuing engagement so that the talent feels supported to do its best. The emotional climate *must* be positive to go full speed.

Give Away Control and Empower People

The verdict is in. People will perform best when they are given control of what they are required to do and empowered to do it. To have the most engaged talent, let them do what you have chosen them to accomplish. Let them do what they are good at doing! Again, the brain knows best. When it is time for the legs to begin walking, the prefrontal cortex, the brain's CEO, hands over control to the subcortical motor system circuitry, such as the basal ganglia, the primary motor cortex, and the cerebellum. At that point, there is minimal prefrontal cortex involvement, since it has its own work to do.

Or think of it this way: As a competitive golfer, when you are under pressure, the trick is to let your body do what it already knows how to do and just hit the shot that you have envisioned. But when fear steps in, you try harder to hit the shot, interfere with your body's movement, and hit it into the lake. The control from the top interferes with the circuitry, causing movement to become slower and much less efficient. This is why when athletes get in the zone, they often describe feeling unconscious of what they are doing.

Similarly, when we do not empower people to control what has been delegated to them, we interfere with their performance. They need to feel free to hit the shot, without the big brain stepping in and interrupting the body part, which knows how to perform. Sometimes, we need focused attention from the top down to correct errors, learn something new, or navigate new information. But most of the time, delegation of control and empowerment to the talent you've chosen, if chosen well, gets the best results.

So, watch out for those moments when you ask someone to do something, and then proceed to "overtell" them how to do it, thus taking away their sense of control and agency. Engaged talent, fully engaged by having control of what they know best, will remain engaged. In Chapters 7 and 8, I'll talk about how measurement and accountability make this more likely to go well.

Create a Positive Emotional Climate

We have seen how safety gets the brain working well. One of the primary reasons is that, when people feel safe, they are fueled by positive chemicals. When they are afraid or hurt, stress hormones and a bunch of other bad stuff flow through their circuits. For the brain and the body to work well, we need great fuel, a positive emotional climate, and nontoxic waste running through our system.

It is up to you to create a climate that feels good. If you do, you'll unleash the higher capacities of your people—logic, judgment, creativity, problem solving, advanced forms of thinking, working memory, planning, the ability to prioritize, big-picture thinking, empathy. All the good stuff will be firing on all cylinders. Plus, studies have shown that moods and negative emotions are just like infections: contagious. A CEO I worked with said that he would tell his people, "If you wake up in a bad mood, stay home. I don't want you bringing that into the office!" Sound like a soft leader? He grew a company to multi-billions from almost nothing. You don't do that by being soft. But you also don't do it if everyone is in a bad mood.

So, you must ask what kind of mood you are creating. Is it inspiring? Positive? Optimistic? Check your tone, your moods, the way you give feedback, and how much optimistic fire you are pushing with the people you are engaging. They need your positive fuel, not negative energy.

As I have mentioned, optimism is critical. We know from decades of research that optimistic people outperform pessimists by a zillion, and they are a lot happier. That doesn't mean that you have to sugarcoat reality or big problems—you must never do that—but you can address them with an optimistic attitude: "We will deal with this and we will conquer it." Make them feel like you are coming alongside them, that you are on the same side of the table with them, and that you are looking at the problem as the enemy, not them. You don't want the talent to fear you. You want them to fear the reality of obstacles or problems and attack them with vengeance. The obstacles are the enemy, and together you will overcome them. As you do this, engagement goes up, and your people get lifted up by your positive force and optimism and go to higher levels themselves. Mood is contagious.

Most visions worth pursuing involve engaging more than one person to achieve them. It takes more than the brain. So always ask yourself: What other talents am I going to need from other people? And how might the particular talent that is needed change and evolve over time? Skills are not fixed in time; necessary new ones can emerge as you start down the path to your desired future. But the question is always alive: What help do I need? From whom will that come?

What About You?

As I've noted, one of the challenges we all face is what I like to call the "default problem." That's when we revert to our usual patterns and try to pursue a vision, build an organization, or find new talent in our own image. What are the limiting beliefs and the inner voices we default to that might be preventing us from engaging talent to realize our vision? Here are some areas to examine:

"I HAVE ALWAYS DONE IT ALL"

In her book *Multipliers*, leadership expert Liz Wiseman describes the difference between "maximizers," who identify what people do best and find ways to amplify it, and "diminishers," who try to control everything and everyone. While you might not consciously think you can do it all, many very responsible, conscientious high achievers operate with the mindset of "it all depends on me." They often grew up that way, go-getters who attacked every task and won every award. These people are so used to feeling like they must do everything, they don't naturally think of what other talent could be empowered to do what is needed. It doesn't even come up on their radar. This can work well for a time, but eventually, you will hit a ceiling and not be able to achieve your goals alone.

My good friend Jim Blanchard, longtime CEO of Synovus, who took a little community bank from $800 million in assets to a combined financial entity now of $62 billion, said that while CEO, he figured out what his job description was each and every day: "I had to figure out what I did that day, and find a way to never have to do it again. I had to find the talent who could do that, so I could focus on going forward."

Overly responsible people tend to dilute their signature strengths and talents by focusing on too many things, and they do not engage other talent to do most of what they are doing that they should *not* be doing. So ask yourself—every day if necessary: What talent is needed to accomplish this, and who could do it better than me? Then you can spend your time doing something where your unique strengths will make a noticeable difference.

And that talent can always be developed. One CEO I worked with grew a big company through acquisitions. He bought smaller ones in the same industry. When we began working together, I saw that finding and evaluating companies was not the best use of his time, and I told him he needed to hand that off to other talent and focus on the real CEO tasks. He had to be involved in every new acquisition, and it was slowing down growth because he was only one person. Their incredible strategy had a ceiling on speed: him.

His immediate response was "I am the only one who can do it like I can. I can see the unrealized value very well and buy them very well. I do it 'instinctively.'"

I told him that I am sure that was true, but what he was calling "instinctive" was actually pattern recognition from having done it so many times. For sure, an experienced hunting dog knows a quail versus a mockingbird. I had him begin to record step by step the thoughts that he had when evaluating a new company and log those. It became clear that there were certain factors that he was putting together instinctively in an instant, but they were still distinct identifiable factors. We put those into a path that he could train a few others to do, and then, he no longer became the brakes on their growth. Now, a handful of years later, the holdings have gone from $30 million to over $500 million in value. The brain found some legs.

"BUT I'VE ALREADY TALKED TO THEM"

A wife said, "You don't tell me you love me, and it hurts." The husband replied, "I told you I loved you when we got married. If it changes, I'll let you know." Not an effective way to keep a person engaged!

Look at your tendency to have a "if it ain't broke, don't fix it" or "squeaky wheel gets the grease" way of engaging or not engaging with talent in a needed cadence. People need to feel connected to you and to the vision. Too often we let our defaults—our habitual relational patterns—play out in our endeavors. If you are a bit of a loner or introvert, for example, some key alliances inside the building and outside might be out of sight and out of mind. You naturally prefer to work alone or just on what you are focusing on. How does that make them feel? Look at the cadence with which your natural wiring engages them. Is it enough? You must offer *just enough*, but *not too much*, input.

Or, some people have the seagull style, as Ken Blanchard puts it: "They fly in, make a lot of noise, crap all over everything, and then fly away." Sometimes, if we are overly critical, the talent only hears from us when there is a problem. Research shows that the human brain needs five to seven positive inputs to metabolize negative criticism. Do you naturally lead with consistency and positivity? To keep walking, a leg must get repeated positive impulses from the brain, not painful shocks. Check your style. You need the right *cadence* of connection, and the right *quality* of connection, enough to stay engaged, and positive enough to keep people engaged.

"AM I SAFE?"

In terms of psychological safety, how safe are you? Look at yourself and maybe even get some feedback on how safe you tend to make people feel. Are you defensive when given feedback? Do you tend to feel criticized instead of helped when people point things out to you? Can they readily disagree or offer a different opinion? Do you instantly counter-debate?

What about when you encounter a failure or mistake? Are you kind or critical when you address it? How is your general emotional climate as you address where someone needs improvement or a different way of doing things? Do they feel valued as they feel corrected?

Do you tend to focus unneeded horsepower on trivial things, in the same way you do on big issues? Do you get just as upset with a small issue as you do a big one? That can create an atmosphere where people walk on eggshells, always afraid of your noticing a mistake. Certainly, you will need to address things that are not where you want them, but not all mistakes are hills to die on. Check on your tendency to major in the minors. Some things just aren't that important, so let them go, or at least address them in a lower-octane manner.

And most importantly, do people feel listened to by you? That is the biggest component of safety, when someone feels "heard" and "seen" and validated before you give your input. If you tend to interrupt or correct others before fully understanding their points, work on slowing yourself down enough to actually listen to what they're saying before reacting.

"AM I A CONTROL FREAK?"

None of us wants to see ourselves as controlling. Often, we are just trying to help or are operating out of fear. We jump in, not knowing we are disempowering people and hurting their performance.

So, do you tend to take over someone's agency or control of something without knowing it? Do you tend to be a back-seat driver? How good are you at letting go? This is hard for many people to consider, and sometimes difficult to hear. It might be helpful to ask others how they see and experience you. If you have created psychological safety with others, they will tell you.

"AM I POSITIVE?"

I once heard a leader ask one of her direct reports sitting around the table, "How are you doing with this?" The guy said, "Good. I'm fine." The leader then replied to him, "Then tell your face."

Check what your face is communicating. Your mood, your tone, your attitude. You might not be aware of it, but sometimes if you are under the gun, you might be allowing negativity to emerge. Gain that awareness. Do you have a tendency to come across negative? Harsh? Disrespectful of others sometimes? Even critical? Are you overly critical of yourself? Get down on yourself? What is good for others is good for you, too. So, ask yourself: *How is my mood? How are my expressions and communications* to myself?

It is hard to feel negative and not reveal it to others. It leaks. If you are struggling with your own negativity and less-than-positive voices in your own head, find someone to help you work those out. They have no place inside you or in the heads of anyone you are engaging to help you get to your *there.*

Moving On

In sum, you create the culture of a team, an organization, a community, and even your family unit. Look at the overall positive emotional climate you are creating with the people who are helping you get *there.* Check yourself to see that you are enlisting the right people to help, keeping in touch with them, empowering them, making them feel safe and optimistic, so that they all can thrive.

That also means checking in with yourself and seeking the growth you need to engage talent and create the culture you want and need.

Now, you have a Vision and the Talent to get you there. Your desired future is to get to the other side of the room, your *there*. You are raring to go, except for one crucial question: "How will you get there?" We will answer that next. But before we do, there is one item worth sharing. We have seen that, after creating a vision, we must engage the talent that is going to help get us there. But here is something important to note. Engaging talent isn't over once you have them on board; sometimes, until you know your strategy, you might not know all the specific talent needed. "Engaging talent" and "creating a strategy" are sometimes a bit of a merry-go-round. So, do not be surprised that engaging talent is going to sometimes continue throughout your trip to *there*, otherwise known as "Finley's Thursday." You, or you and your talent, may come up with a strategy that requires some other talent as well. When you do, remember the points in this chapter, and make sure your strategy has all the talent it needs.

Now, let's look at that next important question: How will we get there?

CHAPTER 5

Strategy: How Will We Get There?

Okay, so you are on one side of the room talking to the group, and your brain comes up with this compelling desired future state of talking to the group from the other side of the room, which would be a lot better than where you are now. *Vision*, check. Done.

Then, your brain realizes it is going nowhere on its own and begins to activate a lot of systems to wake up and get ready for the call to action. Arms, legs, eyes, and so on, as we have seen. *Talent*, check. Done. But nothing has happened yet.

The reason? There is an essential question the body needs an answer to before it springs into action: *How* will we get there?

Think about it. You have options. You could call an Uber, but you quickly determine that it is not a good fit for this mission.

You could ride a pogo stick? Nope. You could skip or roll across the floor? Ride a pony? *Hmmm.* It seems like there are some issues with those, too.

"Wait . . . I got it!" Your brain realizes how after mulling over all possible ways to get to the other part of the room, where the whole audience can see you. "I think I will walk!" It has landed on the answer to the question: *How will we get there?* In life and business, we call that a strategy. It is the answer to the question: *How will I win?*

A Cambridge Dictionary definition of strategy says it well: "a detailed plan for achieving success in situations such as war, politics, business, industry." It answers the question: *How will the vision or goal be achieved?* The way we will get there. And that is what your brain begins to work on from the millisecond the vision is formed. Believe it or not, it is already activating networks of earlier memories, possible resources, obstacles, threats, fears, connections, activities, and so on. All of those are, hopefully, going to add up to, at some point, a cohesive way to get you where you desire to go.

There are two parts to strategy that we will explore. In this chapter, the emphasis is on the *way*. In the next chapter, we will discuss the *how*. Collectively, they form a plan. *The plan is the railway of strategy that will organize the specific actions that will make the "way" be realized in real time and space.*

Winning Takes Strategy

In 2010, Eleven Madison Park hit the Top 50 Restaurants list for the world's best restaurants—an incredible achievement. But as

Will Guidara, the founder, thought about their accomplishment, a question began to capture his attention: "How can we get to #1?"

Naturally, restaurants are known primarily for their food. To get to the top 50, your food must be flawless and, for lack of a better word, *better*. Better than the rest, better than outstanding, and unique in various ways. It must be, as the best of the best are meticulously observed and deeply reviewed. Your food must be seriously amazing to get to the top.

As Will thought about that, he was staring a harsh reality in the face. The top 50 restaurants are *all* awesome in the food category. Every one of them. And each of them always would be. And on top of that, the nuances of awesomeness are almost indistinguishable. Said another way, it is difficult to differentiate yourself as "better" than all the ones who are already "better" than everyone. It's very difficult, and in some ways, very subjective.

As that seemed like an insurmountable task, he asked it a different way. What if there was *another* way to be the best, in addition to having the best food? What if there was a different way to win? A different way to be the best? A different way to get *there*? A different strategy?

His answer? *Be the most hospitable.* In his words (also the title of his book), deliver "unreasonable hospitality." Give diners an experience that is deeply personal and memorable, beyond anything they have ever seen or felt in a restaurant. It would need to be moving, unforgettable, and uniquely, personally crafted for them. What does that strategy look like as it is executed in real life? Here are a few examples:

- A guest was overheard saying that on his visit to NYC, he had been craving a New York–style hot dog off a cart. He was disappointed that he would go home without having had one. So, a staff member ran out of the restaurant and bought hot dogs from a street cart and served them to the guests on a silver tray. Street hot dogs garnished up Michelin style.

- A diner mentioned a favorite dessert from childhood from a bakery that was no longer around. During their dinner, a staff member located a baker to re-create that dessert for the guest before the end of the meal, resulting in the guest crying, having been touched so deeply.

- When a couple got engaged at the restaurant, the staff would serve them champagne in special crystal Tiffany flutes that were different from the other glasses in the restaurant. At the end of the meal, they would present the couple with the glasses they had used to toast their engagement moment, in the famous blue Tiffany box, creating a lasting memory and a gift they would use for a lifetime.

- A couple was overheard saying they had missed their flight for a tropical vacation, so the staff turned a private dining room into a beach getaway, complete with sand and a small pool they could put their feet in, music included.

Unreasonable hospitality became an amazing way to win. Besides what this example illustrates, a successful and winning strategy doesn't always mean just beating someone else. What I mean by "win" is a win for *you*, the accomplishment of *your* goal. A weight-loss win does not mean losing more weight than anyone else in the world. It means accomplishing your vision of health *for yourself.*

When the strategy question gets answered, incredible neurological processes begin to occur. I have mentioned a lot of them, and there are many more that I didn't. One of the key elements of those neurological systems is referred to as the executive function of the brain. More than almost anything, this is what distinguishes humans from Finley. Executive function is the ability to organize resources, energy, planning, options, judgment, actions, and the like along a sequence or timeline that brings about a result. In the highest sense, your executive functions do three things:

1. Attend to what is relevant to get to the vision.
2. Inhibit whatever is not relevant to the vision.
3. Keep the vision and anything relevant in constant awareness along the way, creating a working memory.

That is what a strategy does, *as soon as you name it*. It first defines how you are going to get there, like "walk across the room," as opposed to Uber-ing. It could be "create memorable experiences" for diners in your restaurant. Then it begins to organize *all* your efforts to make sure that your expenditures of energy and your activities are directed to that specific strategy and plan (attending), instead of some other path. These are called *attending* factors. Your executive functions keep you on track and make sure all your efforts are targeted to support your goal, while simultaneously inhibiting other activities or focus from interfering with your progress. Put simply, they keep you saying *yes* to what is important and focusing on it, saying *no* to what is not important (inhibiting), and continuously making you mindful of what you need to do to get there (working memory). Those three are the executive functions of the brain. Your executive functions direct it all: *attending, inhibiting, working memory*.

If your strategy is to walk, you don't stop and sit down along the way or engage in distracting conversations with someone in the front row who asks you a question as you are trying to get across the room. You don't stop and text or order dinner on your phone or scan your e-mail. Your strategy to walk is enabled by your executive functions, which keep you focused on what will get you there until you arrive on the other side of the room as you envisioned. Will's team did not get sidetracked; once their strategy was developed, they stayed focused on delivering unreasonable hospitality above all else.

Strategy not only tells you what to say *yes* to, but it also tells you what to say *NO* to. Most strategy consultants would tell you one of the most important words in strategy is *NO*. Saying *no* is important because you will encounter many bright, shiny objects along the way, all tempting you to stop and admire them. A good strategy reminds you not to get bogged down, not to dilute your energy and draw your focus away from your desired future. We have all heard of companies or individuals described as having "lost their way." They got either sidetracked or diluted.

For example, when a company commits to a strategy of growing their own new locations or branches, it must organize a lot of energy, resources, and activities to make that happen effectively. The focus is, for example, on developing talent that can immediately re-create that brand experience in a new market or location. This is Chick-fil-A's well-known growth strategy, which has made them as incredibly successful as they are. They take their amazing culture and brand consistency into a new location, and from Day One, when the doors open at a new store, a customer will experience the same quality of food and service they have come to expect at Chick-fil-A, regardless of the location. This vision demands that they can scale the level of quality, consistency, and experience their customers expect, but it's their strategy that initiates the results, through a lot of different actions and efforts, such as training and developing people who will be able to execute that kind of cultural and quality consistency. That's their *way* and their *how*. They do it better than most of the scaled restaurant operations in the world. They say yes to things that support the strategy, and no to those that detract from it.

By contrast, if a company's strategy is to grow through acquisitions, which is a very valid strategy for a lot of businesses, then the central idea in their strategy might be to buy every great little chicken restaurant around and convert it into the company brand. The activities—the way and the how—required to implement that strategy would be different from Chick-fil-A's.

Here is another example: I got a call from a regional bank whose growth strategy was moving into new regions by acquiring other smaller banks. The reason they called me was that they recognized their strategy demanded some very intentional activities. They were going to have to integrate all those other banks' cultures into their own and try to make them all have consistent brand experiences for the customer and culture for the employees. They wanted my help in integrating all those banks into one consistent culture.

Neither of these strategies, growth by acquisitions or growth by internally grown expansion, is universally right or wrong. There is no one way to do a growth strategy. But what must be present for all strategies is consistent *effort in prioritized actions*. I'm talking about actions *that move the ball closer to the goal.* Choosing and naming a strategy sets a direction, and then the plan directs the steps into execution. (We will get into the specifics of a plan in Chapter 6.) Here are a few examples of successful strategies that answer the question: "How are we going to get there?"

- Apple: Create an ecosystem for all their products, so customers have multiple products that work together and make leaving the Apple ecosystem difficult.
- IKEA: Keep costs low with furniture built at scale and pass the savings on to customers who are willing to assemble it themselves for that low price.
- Southwest Airlines: Keep costs low (have one model of airplane) and keep turnaround times fast, thus making it cheap and dependable for customers.
- Google: Give away products for free (search, Gmail, maps, Docs, etc.) to get users, and then make money on selling ads for those eyeballs.

In addition to these business examples, notice how strategy works in the rest of life: Your doctor will quickly devise a strategy to reach the vision of curing your infection, and she will execute it with a plan: a particular medicine (strategy) on a particular schedule of dosages (plan). Your kid's teacher will have a strategy to have them reading by the end of the year: phonics learned step by step and applied gradually to reading. A marriage counselor will have a strategy to attack and resolve the issues causing pain in the relationship: emotionally focused therapy weekly with homework and a couples group meeting bi-weekly. Having a plan to execute that strategy brings it to life.

Take weight loss, for example. (Talk about fertile land to discuss strategy.) There are a zillion products, tactics, tips, Instagram reels, and more that people try repeatedly on their own to widely varying degrees of success. But the programs that have worked, and have evidence-based results, have specific strategies. Historically, WeightWatchers (WW) is an example. Clinical research says that it has been more effective over the years than many other programs. (Of course . . . that depends on whether you actually follow the plan.) It has a very specific strategy and plan of execution. Yet interestingly, now, as a *business*, it is losing ground. But before looking at why that is happening, let's look at why the program has worked to help people lose weight.

The WW program had a defined strategy that was built on components that were known to be effective. You can build a strategy around the elements that work in customer experience, or cost savings, for example. The WW strategy for weight loss was constructed around crucial and effective elements: getting people to make healthier food choices, creating behavior change, and implementing a relational support system within a structure. WW built a weight loss strategy with those components all working together. Then, they put those components into a plan that organized specific activities. They came up with a way for people to lose weight that was better than unorganized, hit-or-miss tactics, like when your sister claimed drinking twenty-five glasses of some strange brew worked for her. WW's offer to customers was not an unorganized, random plan. Not only did the WW plan work well for consumers, but it also worked great as a business— until it didn't.

This is where context comes into our discussion of strategy. At the time of this writing, WW's stock is down 80 percent. What happened? WW missed an important detail more recently as it executed its strategy: *context.*

Strategy must always fit the context to reach the vision, to win. Remember the example of walking across the room? We chose walking as a strategy because walking was better than calling an Uber, or skipping, scootering, or rolling, given the context. Walking fits the situation best, and strategy must always fit the situation and context.

When WW was doing well with the model of points to track, in-person meetings, and coaching, it was a different time and place. But in today's context, people are moving to newer digital health platforms. They are bombarded with newer health trends such as keto diets and various apps—not to mention new drugs that promise to replace and outperform most of the components of WW's offerings, which were, let's face it, a lot more demanding of people's time and attention. If WW were beginning today, no doubt they would think differently in the strategy department (as I am sure they are) to adapt to the current context. WW isn't alone in missing out on how the context has changed. It happens all the time—to businesses, entire industries, and to every one of us at some point. Context, context, context. The following are some approaches to help you craft strategies suited to both your personal strengths and the environment in which you'll be working.

SITUATIONAL AWARENESS

This is the task of analyzing the situation that you find yourself in. If you are going to win, your strategy must align and not conflict with your context. For example, when I started my psychiatric hospital company, a "certificate of need" regulation in California was required. That made my initial strategy of starting a brand-new psych hospital pretty much politically impossible to pull off. So, after figuring that out, my new strategy was to buy an existing hospital with financial backing from investors. After raising the money, I still couldn't complete the deal because the existing hospital (and others) I had identified wanted richer buyout terms than my investors and I were prepared to give them. That strategy did not fit the situation. Strike two. So, I had to morph the strategy again to fit the world I found myself in. We then began approaching existing medical-surgery hospitals and converting an underutilized medical wing to a psych ward, partnering with a company that could get us in the door. As I spent more time trying out different strategies, I developed greater situational awareness of the domain, which led me to a different and ultimately better strategy. This took a minute ☺.

But it's not just situational awareness of external factors that matters. We also need to develop situational awareness of internal factors, such as limitations on our time and resources. This is particularly necessary when it comes to strategies around personal health and wellness. A strategy that says I'm going to join a gym to get healthy and requires me to drive to the gym twenty minutes away every morning at 5 a.m. needs to consider my situation—whether I have kids to get ready for school, a dog to walk, or a long commute to work ahead. I must build a strategy to account for these factors. In this case, it might mean riding an exercise bike in my living room while reading work e-mails and watching the kids eat breakfast in the kitchen. The strategy must fit the situation.

USE YOUR STRENGTHS

Fred Smith, the founder of FedEx, was in the military, served two tours in Vietnam, and was awarded a Silver Star, a Bronze Star, and two Purple Hearts. He studied military logistics, which used centralized logistics methods to get things like fuel and supplies from A to B. He used the strengths he learned from the military as he developed a strategy for launching FedEx. If he were a marketing or finance genius, who knows? His strategy might have been different, but he was strong in military logistics, and he used those strengths.

The Philadelphia Eagles used their strengths to win Super Bowl LIX. They employed their impressive defensive line as a key strategy for beating Kansas City by limiting the Chiefs' passing game. The strategy was to stop Patrick Mahomes by applying constant pressure on him and limiting Travis Kelce. They played to their strength, their defensive line.

Steph Curry depends on his strengths of ball handling and shooting to score from the outside. His strategy uses his skills and quickness to create his own shots, often without depending on screens from other players.

Steve Jobs had incredible understanding of how design functions and creating an emotional connection between users and products. Apple's strategy utilized these strengths to stand out from competitors and win customers over based on how something works and how it looks.

If you don't have certain strengths in your professional or your personal endeavors, you must find a way to develop them before you build a strategy that depends on them. Otherwise, you must choose a strategy that utilizes where you can really shine and naturally do well. Or, and this is good news, you can hire the strengths you need or acquire another business that has them.

One useful way to think about your strengths is to identify your value proposition. Great companies differentiate their value proposition by asking: *What can we build or offer that will have unique value to others?* This applies to personal endeavors as well. Ask: *What do I have that brings value?* And see how your strategy will support that.

QUARANTINE YOUR WEAKNESSES

I like to tell people: "You don't need new ways to fail. The old ones are working just fine." This is almost always true. Our weaknesses usually are not situation specific; we often take them with us, endeavor to endeavor. This is why the oft-used SWOT analysis for strategy includes a *W* for *weaknesses*.

However, don't lose heart. The good news is that just because you have a weakness in some areas doesn't mean that it has to take you down. Just protect yourself from your weaknesses. Immunize yourself.

A common scenario we see in personal goals is that someone will devise a strategy that involves a lot of individual discipline. By *individual* I mean tasks or activities that someone is going to have to do on their own and be self-starters to make it happen. That might work if someone's strengths are in creating structure, processes, routines, and schedules. But for someone who operates in a less linear, logical fashion, a self-starter strategy is unlikely to work. It doesn't mean one person is good and the other is bad; it just means that one-size strategies don't exist.

And here's a corollary to that: Don't expect what has never

happened before to happen this time. Bring some structure and discipline to the picture from the *outside*. Hire a trainer! Set up your workouts by making regular appointments with a trainer, joining a group class, or finding a buddy system where your buddy makes you go with them. Or delegate those self-starter functions to someone who likes to do lists and calendars.

If your business strategy depends on a lot of people gathering, and you are a shy introvert, get a wingman or a sales or PR partner in the mix. You need an extrovert to bring people to the table. Success can then come from your knowledge base and ability to persuade the people the extrovert has brought on board, such as customers or investors or whomever. Weaknesses don't have to hold you back—not if you're willing to bring on someone with complementary strengths as a counterbalance. Do what you do well, and don't let your weaknesses keep your strengths from being properly utilized. An important note here: You know that "engaging talent" is not a one-time effort (see Chapter 4). Sometimes the strategy we devise demands new talent that was not on board earlier.

If your strategy is to develop a new business in an area where you're not already strong, you can build strength through an acquisition. For example, in 2012, Facebook was weak in mobile photo sharing, and they could see that a younger population was going more mobile. Instagram was dominating that area, so Facebook acquired them, which gave them stronger mobile engagement, and protected them from a declining user base. These days, Instagram represents a big chunk of Meta's revenue.

The lesson is that you don't have to be killed by your weaknesses. Acquire strength where you are weak, and thus immunize your strategies. Think back to Tom Brady building his new team. Or Apple, which was weak in product design for a while, until they hired Jony Ive. Microsoft was weak in cloud computing and mobile, and hired Satya Nadella as CEO, who was strong in cloud computing.

Your weaknesses will kill your great strategy unless you seek and find strengths in others.

DETERMINE THE OBSTACLES

The T in a SWOT analysis stands for *threats*. That speaks directly to these vital questions: When you have your vision, what stands in the way of your getting there? What might block its success? Identify those factors as you develop your strategy and find ways to deal with them or render them irrelevant. They might include things such as technological disruptions, market shifts, new regulations, emerging consumer trends, political shifts, and so forth. They should all be on the radar screen, like the weather patterns on a pilot's display screen. Netflix saw streaming coming directly to the TV and moved away from DVDs just in time.

In many cases, the T in a SWOT could also stand for *technology* since many of the changes disrupting business and personal lives are related to technology. Anyone who is in the business of digital content today faces an obstacle, a pervasive "threat." You used to be able to develop great content, put it on the web, and sell it to people. But increasingly, content is ubiquitous. Anyone can find YouTube videos on pretty much anything for free. That is a real obstacle to charging for content in many subject areas today.

While people may be reticent to pay for content, they will pay for *curating* and *organizing* content. Sites that have structured courses with quality curation of subjects or experts have found a compelling value proposition. For example, you can find most of the subjects in Masterclass in a variety of other places if you're willing to spend time searching for the best stuff. But Masterclass has done the work for you by curating some of the best, organizing it into very usable forms, and giving people an easy-to-find place for learning. That's not only their strategy, it's the value proposition that makes them distinctive in a crowded marketplace for content. This is also what my Leadership University (Leadu.tv) does for companies. I bring together the best leadership content into a structured leadership training program that companies and individuals can use, instead of having to go on a wild-goose chase themselves to find it. If you check out my personal growth online platform, you will find the same curating strategy. Both can be found at drcloud.com.

CONTROL WHAT YOU CAN CONTROL

A formula for failure is to depend on things *outside of your control*. If your wedding planning business depends on only producing outdoor weddings, and you want to open in Seattle, you have a problem unless you can control the weather, or unless your strategy accounts for this out-of-your-control factor. For example, you could build an alliance with venues that have great outdoor spaces and an available tent for 300 people if it rains that day. The weather you can't control won't derail you if your strategy plans for it.

If I were going to treat a patient and their illness with a

medication that must be taken every day at a specific time, my success in treating them would be dependent on their ability to remember to take the pill exactly as prescribed. So, if they do not have that ability, I need to make sure they are in a structured environment or have a buddy system in place so that my treatment strategy can be implemented. My strategy must be constructed knowing what it is I can control but also what mechanisms and structures need to be put in place for things outside my control.

In the financial meltdown of 2008, the free-falling economy was outside the control of the financial industry. Finding new clients and getting more investment from them was being affected by an out-of-control economy. I headed a project with 8,000 brokers and financial advisors, where we systematically defined a host of activities within their control that could be executed with clients. Making structured plans, getting groups of clients together, coming up with lists of activities that were in the advisors' total control turned their performance around and got them out of the paralysis that being out of control was engendering. By focusing on what they could control, they were successful.

A winning strategy accounts for both the factors and activities that can be controlled as well as those that can't. Otherwise, you will just have to keep hoping it doesn't rain.

Front and Center

One more crucial reminder: Strategy cannot be just a passing thought. It is an organizing principle of the entire endeavor. It pulls what may look like disparate parts together in one direction, with everyone's awareness and emphasis placed on the same spot. As with our brains, a good strategy keeps the working memory busy. It loads attention and inhibits distraction. Message, message, message, repeatedly. Put stickers up, create regular intervals of communication with your teams, the entire enterprise, and sometimes even your outside alliances. Embed these messages in everything you do.

In the same way that the body's movement across the room seems like it's happening at an unconscious level, your desired future—if it's backed by a specific strategy that engages all the talent you need with clarity—will start to feel almost as natural as a walk across the room. But don't be fooled—it takes work and a real plan to get where you want to go. We'll turn to this fourth element—the plan—in Chapter 6.

What About You?

Just as we saw with vision and engaging talent, identifying your personal strengths and weaknesses is vital. We can shore up personal weaknesses by creating more structure and enlisting support from others who have complementary strengths. During strategy formulation, a different set of personality traits may come into play, and those are harder to change because they involve deeply rooted cognitive styles—the diverse ways individuals perceive, think, remember, and, most importantly, problem solve. These tend to be more fixed, with some cognitive styles being more adaptive to strategic thinking, whereas others are more suited to tactics and operations.

I have worked with *many* CEOs who had incredible strategic minds. Once they had a vision, they instantly saw how to get there—they could visualize all the moving parts, conditions, and necessary steps to make it happen. They intuitively saw the connections from beginning to end. That's one kind of cognitive style. But I've also worked with other executives and team members who, upon hearing a big vision, find themselves befuddled and consumed with questions about the *how*. They need to understand the steps and tactics to engage with the strategy. So you can imagine what might happen when the two cognitive styles come together for a strategy session. One is already seeing the finish line; the other is staring into a black hole, wondering what their colleague is talking about.

There are as many ways to categorize cognitive styles as there are assessment tools to pinpoint yours. Naturally, most of us don't use one single style; we blend several, leaning into one style over the other, depending on the circumstances. So, with that hefty grain of salt, let's look at a few styles:

- **Big-picture thinkers:** World-class chess players don't just focus on the pieces on the board; they also see the whole board several moves ahead. As Wayne Gretzky famously said, "I skate where the puck is going to be, not where it has been." To do that, you must look at the whole field of play, not just the player in front of you. Big-picture types are intuitive, seeing patterns and openings that others miss, but they may also think too abstractly, overlook the details, and miss or minimize risks.

- **Analytical thinkers:** People like this use data, logic, and reasoning, and can break problems into parts and then evaluate the trade-offs. They are extremely helpful in ensuring that a plan is realistic, not just visionary. They anticipate issues that will emerge ahead of time. The weakness of analytical thinking is commonly referred to as analysis paralysis. This style of thinking is slower and may make someone reticent to act.

- **Integrative thinkers:** These types of thinkers see opposites and can reconcile differences to come up with creative solutions to seemingly unsolvable conflicts. They can find ways to balance competing dynamics and somehow make everything work. They bring together things that conflict with one another and find a third way. At the same time, integrative thinkers may overcomplicate things or become overly ambitious, spending too much time trying to reconcile it all.

- **Adaptive thinkers:** People with this style have the capacity to adjust strategy when things change and are quick to test assumptions. In the face of obstacles, they pivot quickly, finding workarounds and detours to get to their destination. They can also be indecisive and get caught up in perpetual reevaluation. Sometimes they waver too much and can't stick with an idea.

- **Reactive thinkers:** Reactive thinkers respond well in a crisis, but tend to focus on the present and its immediate problems. They respond to what is right in front of them, doing well under pressure and with deadlines, but they may miss the bigger picture and the ramifications of short-term actions.

- **Detailers:** Detailers are great at execution, tactics, systems, and processes. But they may also be too narrow in their scope and can get bogged down by trying to tie a bow on every detail before moving on to other things.

- **Relational thinkers:** People with this style prioritize relationships, alliances, collaboration, and communication. They build great teams and culture, but they may not pay sufficient attention to the work itself.

These are just some of the common ways of thinking about your thinking. The main point I want you to see here is that you must look at yourself and avoid having a strategy built "in your own image." You must consider which cognitive styles might be missing and ensure they are included in the mix as you devise the strategy to determine how you will win. Knowing your own cognitive style will make you a better leader and someone more likely to reach your vision and desired future in general, and it will help you avoid some of the pitfalls that stop great strategies from coming to fruition.

BEWARE OF FRUSTRATION

It is not unusual for someone to have a great idea and vision, but feel very stuck as they begin to think, "How will I get there?" There seems to be no straight line to get from here to there, even though their idea is a winner.

Sometimes, they will begin to take steps, then revert to the way they've always done it. Despite having a vision, talent, and strategy, they wind up behaving like Finley, who does the same things every day. Finley doesn't have a vision, talent, or strategy, but she gets the same results as someone who has those things but cannot act on them.

When your tried-and-true methods don't work, feelings of helplessness, frustration, and impatience can emerge. For big-picture types—those who see the vision and the finish line all at once—feelings of frustration may set in when others get mired in details (which they probably consider minutiae). And for the tactical types—those who need to work out all the steps and answer all the questions to see a way forward—the big-picture types may seem like nothing more than big talkers, who don't appreciate the challenges they'll face in implementing their vision.

Being confronted with a different style can produce a feeling of "why bother?" If you start to feel impatient and frustrated, it's okay. It may mean you need to slow down to explain the thinking behind your thinking, or it may mean you need to speed up, deferring detailed questions to a subsequent session when a call for action (a plan!) is needed. You also need to appreciate that styles other than yours are beneficial to the strategic exercise. Ask yourself: What can I learn from another approach? What might I be missing? Don't let the feeling of helplessness stop you; they might just be a signal that you need another style with you.

BEWARE OF BLIND SPOTS

If you do a SWOT strategy analysis, which looks at strengths, weaknesses, opportunities, and threats, and just hop out to build a strategy "in your own image, Finley," then watch out. I have seen leaders who *think* they have a particular strength, but they do not. They begin to execute and fail because they thought they had strengths, or thought someone in the company had them, but they were wrong.

I remember one CEO of a public company who ran a division very, very successfully. Finally, he got tired of making millions for the company and wanted to go out on his own. What he failed to see was that the strategy to win depended on building very strong processes and systems. But he had been successful in operating a company that *already* had those in place, so he didn't see the gap. He had never designed and built systems. At the big companies where he worked, they were already there. Though he had a highly successful history, he failed at the new venture and lost all his investors' money. Millions. He didn't see what was missing to accomplish the strategy until it was too late.

Don't let your past success in other contexts make you think you can just keep doing one thing over and over again. Take an inventory of the strengths needed, in you or someone else. Talk to others who have the cognitive style and know-how to recognize what the strategy will need along the way, and ask them to weigh in.

I learned this the hard way once with a company I built on my own. I had previously succeeded with great operational people alongside me, and I provided other strengths. But when I began the new venture, I was off and running, without thinking about operations. The company was doing well, and it grew into a larger business, but the operations were a mess, and they were key to the vision. The vision was strong, I was able to attract and engage talent, and my strategy was a great one, but the strategy depended on a lot of structured operational capacity that I did not have. After digging myself into a hole, I cried uncle, came out of denial, and found a great operator to work with me. From there, things went well. Since then, I have started and built a few other enterprises that have done well because, after getting a strong vision and beginning to look at strategy, *the first thing I do is find the operator*!

BEWARE DENIAL

Another place personality might play a role is when someone's style is to deny weaknesses and overvalue strengths. Being an optimist and thinking the best of people is an admirable trait, until it causes someone to lose touch with reality. It is quite common for a leader to see a particular person in their organization through rose-colored glasses and think that they can do nothing wrong. The leader is blind to the ways in which that person is not a superstar in *every* way. A common example is a great number-two person who becomes a CEO but just doesn't have it. When it comes to strategy, be honest about how your players fit the strategic process and whether their cognitive style is suited to it. Find ways to assess whether they have the personality and aptitude to take on a new role without simply throwing them into the deep end or asking them to think like you.

BEWARE OF THE BUBBLE

I know a leader who has started several enterprises, and each one of them begins pretty quickly, gets some speed, and then hits a ceiling. Why? Every time, he tends to begin by going to the people already in his network. He lives in and depends on a small pond, when there are literally oceans that he does not consider.

As we have discussed earlier, it is important to get out of your known world of "how to win." This also means looking beyond your known world of relationships. You may be missing huge pieces of strategy that you have never seen done before, and people who could offer tremendous help, if only you knew they existed. Your biggest growth step might involve becoming less dependent on the people you already know, copying things you and they have done before, and focusing more on exploring people, domains, and experiences that are entirely new to you.

A lot of strategic errors happen due to a lack of humility and curiosity. The lack of humility is the tendency to think that we know everything that is necessary and possess all the pieces to make it work. We just begin doing everything as we've always done it, like Finley, running to the door and barking. In the presence of humility, we take an honest look at what we are good at, what we know, and how we think, assessing how that matches up with our strategic needs. When we see gaps, we have the humility to say, "I need some other eyes and voices in here."

Lack of curiosity occurs when we think we know all there is to know. We don't consider the myriad ways of doing things that we don't know about. We disregard the unknown unknowns that are readily available to us if we could actively go out and learn. It takes humility and curiosity to learn, and the benefits of both are huge.

One of the things that endeared me greatly to one of my team members who oversaw digital marketing was the day I asked him about a particular area of data analysis. I asked, "Do you know all that we need to know about it? Are we doing all that we need to be doing? Are you sure about that?" He answered, "I know a lot. But I think I probably know about 80 percent of what we need to know." My heart leaped for joy and appreciation for him at that moment, for both his humility and his curiosity. We immediately went and found the other 20 percent outside the company, and it took us to a whole other level.

Get out of your bubble.

BEWARE OF THE NOW

One other weakness you might want to check for is the tendency to want it all right now, too soon. That can be a great trait because it means you are likely to take action. You want to get moving. Go for it! That's awesome, and we need "go for it" people. The problem is that action-prone people tend to leap before checking the altimeter to see if the plane is high enough for a parachute to open in time. Instead of "ready, aim, fire," they are "fire, aim, ready."

When devising or changing a strategy, if you have what seems like a great idea, you might need to do some pilot tests. As Jim Collins says, fire bullets instead of cannonballs. Take little steps first to see if they work, tweak them until they do, or abandon them to find the right ones. In a lot of situations, acting immediately is critical, but in launching a new strategy, you can also take little practice runs before betting the farm on an untested idea. Test small, evaluate, adapt.

Moving On

Successful people know how they are going to win, and then execute that strategy relentlessly. They adapt it as they go along, sticking to it until it no longer fits the lay of the land. They do not just go for it without a strategy and a plan. Otherwise, efforts are scattered and diluted when a laser focus is required.

But, as we've discussed here, strategy must also be executed along a timeline that identifies what's required operationally—what specific actions and steps must happen when, and who is going to do what. That is the railway of strategy, the plan. It is what the brain begins to come up with as soon as you name a vision and strategy. The brain is already planning to plan. In the next chapter, we will see how a plan is put into place and executed to help you reach your desired future.

CHAPTER 6

The Plan: What Every Strategy Needs

If you lived in the 1800s, and you wanted to sail from Colón, Panama, to Balboa, Panama, it would take you eight months to travel approximately 15,000 miles by sailing around Cape Horn on the southern tip of South America. That is, if you made it. Those are treacherous waters with some of the roughest seas on Earth. If you made it, you had survived fifty-foot waves, horrible visibility, and hidden ice, ready to sink your ship. This journey was known as the "sailor's graveyard" because of the thousands of shipwrecks along the route.

That's why people dreamed of building a canal across the Isthmus of Panama, the narrow strip of land that connects North America and South America. If your vision was to be a world power or remain one, to dominate commerce through slashing shipping time and costs, as well as other benefits, a great strategy would be to build a canal across that isthmus.

Since at least the 1500s, people had dreamed of crossing by land, but Spain surveyed the route and realized crossing the isthmus was impossible. How would anyone get from *here* to *there*? So, people kept going the long way. What about a canal? People considered it, but it never happened. The canal remained a pipe dream for a couple of hundred years. What a vision, what a strategy, if only it could be done!

Enter Count Ferdinand de Lesseps of France, a canal builder who built the Suez Canal in Egypt, joining the Mediterranean and Red Seas, reducing sailing distances between Europe and East Asia. So, why not here in Panama? Building a canal made sense to him, so he tried.

What happened was disastrous. De Lesseps and his team immediately tried to connect from sea level to sea level, but it was too difficult. The terrain made it impossible. They considered locks before abandoning that idea. Equally difficult as these feats of engineering was the task of keeping workers alive. The rains and heavy landslides that made construction horribly difficult also fueled a breeding ground for mosquitoes. Yellow fever and malaria killed around 22,000 workers. It proved too much, and the French abandoned the effort.

But the opportunity did not go away. Enter another leader, Theodore Roosevelt. His approach to turn the US into a military and economic global power is one of the best examples of translating a vision into a strategy, and that into a plan. Today we have the Panama Canal. Perhaps it was Roosevelt's philosophy that fueled him to start: "Far better it is to dare mighty things, to win glorious triumphs, even though checkered by failure, than to take rank with those poor spirits who neither enjoy much nor suffer much, because they live in the gray twilight that knows not victory or defeat." *But how? Why was he able to accomplish the vision when others had failed in the very same context?* Short answer: He did it like the human body does it.

I wondered about that question as I was putting together Leadership University, my online leadership development course (LeadU.tv). I became so interested in the *contrast* between Roosevelt's winning approach and the French team's failure that I flew to Panama to interview the premier historian of Panama, Vladimir Berrio-Lemm. I wanted his account of how the same vision and the same context could produce two wildly different results. Here is what he told me, edited for brevity: "Ferdinand had a dream. A big dream, but not a vision. When you have a vision, you have a plan. A dream is up there [pointing up to the sky], not down to earth." The historian went on to explain that de Lesseps had engaged the wrong people and ran into problems. He explained that Roosevelt had a vision and a *plan*. He also had the talent: a chief engineer and a physician to fight the diseases. He engaged the right people and delegated to them in an orderly and disciplined manner. He executed his plan by allowing the right people to make decisions, which they did correctly, and they followed a plan, which made his dream a reality (see LeadU.tv for the full interview).

As Vladimir answered my questions, I was struck by how this example illustrated the path to the desired future that I'm describing in this book. First comes the vision; then, recruiting the talent. For example, Roosevelt recruited chief engineer John Frank Stevens, who other historians have explained "approached the construction of the canal more systematically than the early, almost random efforts" by both the French and the Isthmian Canal Commission. (See Maurer, Noel, and Carlos Yu. *The Big Ditch: How America Took, Built, Ran, and Ultimately Gave Away the Panama Canal*, Princeton University Press, 2010, 100.) I love that phrase—*random efforts*—because it perfectly illustrates what happens to a vision without a plan.

Plans are anything but random. They align all energy with the strategy, which draws upon the vision. Roosevelt's engineer, Stevens, designed and worked on a plan dispatching talent to activities in a systematic order. Stevens began by examining the context and obstacles that the plan would have to address, starting with the threat of disease to workers. He hired the world's leading expert on yellow fever, Dr. William Gorgas, to eliminate the diseases transmitted by the mosquitoes. Stevens also halted digging—those random efforts—to develop a workable plan. From there, Stevens began to execute a lock-canal plan that would connect the two oceans. He carefully sequenced every step with diligence, establishing specific milestones to gauge progress: eradicate disease, rebuild infrastructure around the construction zone to get construction materials, build living quarters for thousands of workers, develop supply lines, impose military style management structures, and on and on. Meanwhile, Roosevelt took *political* steps to help the plan along the way, including supporting Panama's independence in exchange for US rights to control the canal.

When Stevens stepped away from the project, Roosevelt appointed a military man who structured the rest of the undertaking with military precision, overcoming most of the same problems the French had faced. It wasn't a matter of random luck; it was a victory, a great accomplishment of massive engineering, borne out of a winning strategy and a bulletproof plan.

The problem with so many efforts in personal lives and business is that, while someone has a vision and even a strategy, they are missing a railway for it to stand on: the plan. So, what is a *plan*?

Plan Essentials

Vision tells us where we are headed and why (our desired future), and strategy tells us the *way* we will get there; the plan puts the *how* into the *way*, the *strategy*. As Berrio-Lemm said, it brings the vision "down to reality on the earth." It tells us how we will win by showing us what we will do. A vision is a future state in our heads, but combining strategy with a plan turns the vision into a present state that will exist in real life. That requires action. The plan outlines what has to be done—the activities that move the needle—who will do what, when they will complete it, and what resources will be applied to the effort. Plus, the plan articulates clear ownership of those actions and results. All of this is organized along a timeline that breaks down the necessary activities into small, sequential steps. Without a plan, a strategy remains a concept. With a plan, it gets operationalized. A strategy without a plan is ambition, and a plan without strategy is noise. They need each other.

While a strategy sets direction, a plan defines the milestones that must be met on a timeline. Remember the home builder from Chapter 4 who wanted to complete his projects with greater speed to increase profit margins? His plan put the subcontractors' work onto a cohesive timeline. You have a plan when you know exactly how to put your resources into action by establishing who does what and when.

This organizes the priorities of the strategy into a sequence, which is a key aspect of the executive functions that transform a desire into a set of actions. As with the human brain, a strategic plan sequences the actions, allowing us to *attend* to what is relevant, *inhibit* what is distracting, and, all the while, keep the vision in the forefront of *working memory*. Another way to put it: The plan is the structure that strategy needs in order to be realized.

The plan also structures milestones and expectations. If Chick-fil-A is going to grow its revenue from within by injecting its culture into new locations, many things need to happen: Its real estate team must find locations and get them ready to go. Its human resources and training team needs to prepare employees for assignments in those new locations. Its operations team needs to sort out logistics to ensure they have the supplies they need and can keep the counter and the drive-through moving. That is a *lot* of activity along a sequenced timeline with many "who does what by when" pieces. And none of that is random effort, as Stevens proved. Rather, it's a matter of nailing down only those things that are relevant to the goal. In the end, you have a goal with defined actions and milestones, people who own responsibility for them, a way to hold everyone accountable for them, and a method to track everything along the way. If milestones are missed, you must have established corrective actions as part of your plan. (We will dive into those in Chapters 8 and 9.)

This creates a virtuous circle: The psychological energy required to execute the plan increases performance, and the achievement of milestones increases the positive psychological energy to press on. In other words, *not only does the structure ensure everything gets done, but the getting it done and the performance itself are empowered by the plan's structure and presence.* Leadership, as I wrote in *Boundaries for Leaders,* is only successful when leaders lead in the ways that human brains can follow. In the same way that a plan triggers the brain's executive functions, a strategic plan triggers the "executive functions" of your team—activating the doers, the implementers, the operators. It's like double-clicking on an app that causes people to perform by providing clarity and getting rid of the biggest impediment to performance: ambiguity. It also reduces two of the biggest performance killers, the wrong kind of stress and inaction.

When people's brains are stressed by a lack of focus, indecision, and confusion, it signals the release of stress hormones like cortisol. In fact, research has shown that stress can reduce IQ by 15 points or more! If you want the best creativity, judgment, decision making, and performance, you want people's brains to be filled with dopamine and other chemicals instead of cortisol. In the same way that schedules and incremental steps can calm down little kids and reduce their ADHD-like behavior, structure can calm us down. The right amount of structure is absolute gold.

In *Boundaries for Leaders,* I said that every employee should be able to answer one question every day: "What activities am I doing today, and how do those activities directly move the needle to accomplish what we are trying to do?" Great plans accomplish this, ensuring that employees are energized, motivated, and clear about what they are supposed to do. Furthermore, when milestones are hit, it creates momentum. One of the key motivators of performance is the awareness and feeling that "we are making progress!" It is huge, and only a plan can clearly show this to people day to day. It makes their days worth the effort.

Amazon's strategy was embedded in their statement to "become the Earth's most customer-centric company, where customers can find and discover anything they want to buy online." You can see the plan in the strategy's sequence of ideas. By building everything around customer convenience, like low prices, vast selection, and fast delivery, they can meet the first part of the strategy. From there, they focused on the infrastructure that would deliver that, building state-of-the-art fulfillment centers and warehouses. Then they streamlined the buying experience and added global expansion with localization. It all comes down to the details—the "who, what, when" activities that had to be organized to pull that off in each step.

This is equally true for personal goals, even for this book, for example. Authoring books on leadership and personal growth is part of my mission, but a long time ago I had to learn *how*. It seemed daunting when an organization first asked me to write a book on my training content. I had no idea how to write a book, but I did have a vision for it. As I've made the case in these pages, my vision (to write a book) needed to engage the right talent to help me. So, the organization hired a consultant to walk me through a strategy of writing and marketing, both of which I still use. The strategy consists of gathering content over time based on my daily work with leaders, teams, and organizations, and by studying research. The material that goes in the book needs to be relevant and proven to work. Next, I need to organize it and give it some structure. It contains many of the ingredients of a plan you might develop for your business or your personal goals. Here are some components of my plan for writing this book after the initial gathering of content and organizing it:

Step 1: I meet with my agent and share the content with her, and she takes it to my publisher to get them to weigh in. I then also meet with my publisher to discuss the direction of the book.

Step 2: I land on an agreement with the publisher as to what the book will cover. At that point, we sign a contract and set a deadline. I agree to deliver around 60–70,000 words by a certain date.

Step 3: I create an Excel spreadsheet showing, week by week, how many words I need to write to have 70,000 words by the due date. I include about a month for me to revise and edit the material.

Step 4: I match the word count needed per week with blocks of time on my calendar to get it done in chunks.

Step 5: I organize the file with all the material I've collected over the time I was planning to write the book. I come up with a list I call "keepers," ideas, concepts, research, and illustrations that will end up in the book.

Step 6: I organize the "keepers" into an outline for chapters, including headings and supporting material.

Step 7: I begin writing, being sure to hit my weekly word count targets, and send the finished chapters to a few "readers" who give me feedback. I weigh that feedback against my vision and integrate what is helpful.

Step 8: Celebrate!! I am now done. I've sent all the chapters to my publisher and await feedback about edits and changes. I create a similar timeline to review the edits and fix things, which goes pretty quickly.

Over the years, many people have told me, "I would love to write a book." I hear that a lot. And then I ask, "So, why don't you?" Most of the time, the answer I get is "I don't have time." I like to be respectful, but inside I often think, "So what? I don't either." With few exceptions, I have never taken time off to hole up and write a book, like many authors do. I am a practitioner, not an "author," in my mind. I work full-time. I have a day job. I "don't have time" to write books.

But I have also written a lot of books. How? Exactly like I just said. For decades, I have used a structured plan that makes it all possible. The structured plan literally *finds time*. Planning is almost like a time machine that creates time because it uses the time you have in the most effective way. Without it, I would be lost, as I am not a very structured person by nature. Having a plan makes it all possible.

Another example comes from author John Grisham, who was an attorney and a member of the Mississippi House of Representatives, who had always wanted to write a book but "didn't have time." So, he got a plan: He got up an hour early and wrote one page a day. In two years, he had written *A Time to Kill*, and since then, he has written dozens of other books, many of them adapted for the big screen and streaming services.

Simple, right? It's not rocket science by any measure, and it's nowhere near as complicated as building Amazon, but it still requires a plan with similar components. The specifics of your plan will obviously depend on your goal, but the *necessity* for a plan and its components are nearly universal. Even getting the kids to school or in bed on time requires a plan! (In my experience, that is harder than authoring a book.)

The human body delivers results in an ordered sequence, with the brain's executive functions releasing focused energy and resources at the right time in the chain. Certainly, stuff happens, and there is ongoing adaptation to changing circumstances, but we still need to get there on time.

A great manufacturing term that relates to a plan is the *critical path*. A critical path is defined as the longest sequence of dependent tasks that must be completed on time for the project to finish on time. If you are going to get something done, there is always some linear process involved, and the most straightforward way for that to happen is to have a plan that defines who does what by when. The gate system in manufacturing is a similar idea. Everyone must complete their piece and meet approval checkpoints (called *gates*) before moving to the next phase. In terms of the human body, one foot must be on the ground before the other leg is lifted, or you'll lose your balance and fall. Your plan needs those kinds of gates—steps, checklists, milestones—too.

The Plan Puts It All Together

Strategy tells us where we want to go, and the plan dictates how the strategy will actually occur, what the activities will be, by whom, and by when. It puts all the components together using a timeline. It also assigns roles and responsibilities to individuals and teams, and clarifies who is accountable for each. (We will examine the accountability portion in the next chapter in detail.)

A winning plan also ensures that all activities align with the strategy. For everything we are doing, there *must* be an explanation of why. The answer must be that each activity advances the strategy to realize the vision. With alignment comes the need to look at resources: how money, time, and people will be injected into the steps of the plan at the right intervals. It is no good showing up for battle without any bullets.

Peter Drucker is credited with saying "Nothing is more worthless than doing the wrong things perfectly." Inherent in this comment is the need for what I've called *pruning.* (See my book *Necessary Endings.*) Just as important as putting the right components into the plan is getting rid of components that inhibit it. As noted, this is what your brain does, too. Some pre-existing practices might dilute energy and resources, so ask yourself: *Does this move the needle on our strategy?* If not, ask yourself, *Why are we doing it? Would a customer care that you did something, or is it superfluous? Would it make the project any better?* If not, it might have to go. Sacred cows have no place if they are living on the wrong farm. One of my mentors told me always to ask two questions: "Why am I doing that?" and "How can I do it better?"

When Stuff Happens

A plan has a timeline created to get you to *there.* But stuff happens. It is guaranteed. Chapter 7 discusses how to minimize stuff happening, and how to recover from it, but for now just remember that every good plan, while pushing for accountability, also accounts for misses and assumptions that might need to be recalibrated along the way. I address this as the last step on the path to your desired future (Chapter 9). That doesn't necessarily mean moving the goalposts or deadlines, but it probably does mean adjusting and fixing some of the activities of your plan *before* the deadline gets close. You have to somehow make up for lost time, so conduct an ongoing review to look at your plan and adjust the activities and milestones, and their timing, along the way, without moving the final deadline. For example, when I'm writing a book and I miss my word count number for a particular week for some unexpected reason, I have to look ahead on my calendar and probably get rid of something of a lower priority so that I can spend that time writing. The only likely way to find more time is by pruning something else from next week's schedule. That's why when a plan is being formulated, it's helpful to build in a margin of safety—extra time, money, or resources to prevent the schedule from running in the red all of the time. If you have ever remodeled a house, you have learned this! Make room for some white spaces, just in case. Said another way, if Google Maps tells you it is going to take forty-five minutes to get to the airport, that might be true only if there are no wrecks on the freeway. The wise person leaves an hour for the trip instead of forty-five minutes. We can never assume that things will go smoothly. Plan for things to go wrong. The fifteen minutes of padding will be better spent in the airport lounge than freaking out on the freeway, knowing you will miss a flight ☺. Remember, a plan reduces stress.

What About You

We have talked about how our personal makeup, our tendency to bark like Finley, can interfere with the essentials. When setting our vision, we saw that we might be limited in our ability to think big enough. While engaging the talent, we saw how personal issues might keep us from effectively pursuing our goal. When determining strategy, the same thing applies. Our cognitive styles might limit our potential to achieve our desired future, so it is no surprise that the same is true when it comes to the plan. There are a few important things to consider.

ARE YOU CLOSURE ORIENTED OR OPEN ENDED?

If you have ever taken a personality assessment such as the Myers-Briggs, they will tell you that some people, like those who score high on Judging, are very closure oriented and love clear deadlines, structured linear approaches (like a plan), and timelines. They love to check things off as done. "Ah, what that must be like!" says a P (Perceiving) like me. Others, like me, are not closure oriented and automatically see the world differently. We are more process oriented, flexible, and adaptable, comfortable with loose ends and exploring along the way. That leads to more creativity and enables us to do a lot of different things and have a lot going on at once. But you can see the problem. We still must finish a book on time, or we suffer or cause suffering for ourselves and others.

Honestly, we don't always need assessment tools to tell us what type we are; our spouses, teachers, friends, and others can easily tell us. And it is vital to know because it makes us aware that, if we do not face our preference for open-endedness and deal with it, we will leave a lot of loose ends dangling. I had to learn this early in my career, when dealing with many hard deadlines. This approach did not come naturally to me, and I struggled to avoid missing details. I even forgot to renew my psychologist license early on in my career, the consequence of which was that I had to have someone with a license accompany me on clinical visits for a week, until I got it renewed. Ouch. It was embarrassing and expensive to do the actual therapy, because I could not bill for those visits!

Some deadlines cannot be missed, so you must find systems to ensure *you realize that a plan is needed first*! You will not naturally drift towards making one, but you must. Obviously, a plan won't turn me into a Myers-Briggs J rather than a P, but a good plan makes up for my weaknesses. I now use plans *a lot* to make up for what I do not do naturally. And I am relieved to say, I have never missed another licensure renewal or book deadline. If a plan can work for me, it can work for anyone!

You can use systems, and you can use other people's help. When I hired my assistant, I told her, "Your main job description could be chief nagging officer. I will have so much stuff going on and not be aware of a deadline that you will have to nag me to get it done." She and I have a real-time, shared digital note that we update, sometimes throughout the day. That's just one example of a tool that prevents me from falling off my plan.

DO YOU HAVE THE RIGHT MIX ON YOUR TEAM OR IN YOUR CIRCLE?

As you are putting together your talent, look around the table. Is it a bunch of Ps and no Js? Where are the structured doers?

Where are the operators? Do you have enough creatives or too many? Where are your number crunchers and analytical types? Do you have a chief nagging officer if you need one? Or a chief challenge officer? Check the ingredients to get the right mix.

As we noted in Chapter 5, some of these folks might drive you crazy at times; others may strike you as being pedantic or nitpicky. That's not their problem—it's yours to address. Overcome any tendency to see them as a pain in the you-know-what, learn to love them, and thank God for them. Stop judging them and be grateful for the value they can add. At times, give the talented, unstructured people the structure and support they need to compensate for their weaknesses. Bosses finally face the music and understand they are wasting salespeople's talents by asking them to complete a lot of follow-up paperwork when their real talents are people-oriented, aggressive sales work. Another way to put it: Don't try to teach a pig to sing. Find someone else to sing showtunes and, while you are hiring talent, add someone to clean up the sty. Planning *must* be done, so if you don't naturally gravitate to it, assign someone to oversee this critical step. One of my client companies, an extraordinarily successful one, has a planning group of thirty people who take the executive team's strategies and make a linear plan to get them done. God gave us days, weeks, months, and years for a reason.

DO YOU HAVE A DRI?

I have a quick word about the importance of the directly responsible individual (DRI). Steve Jobs is credited with this term; he would often ask, "Who is the DRI?" The DRI is the *one person* responsible for making sure this task or project gets done. Think of how many times something is lagging in the plan, leaving you to play a game of telephone tag to find out why. You talk to one person who says it is another department's fault, they are waiting on finance to send the budget, or some other form of "the dog is still chewing on my homework." Assigning a DRI to the parts of the plan ensures that *ownership is clear*. That way, the plan can keep moving quickly because there is only one person to talk to. There is a reason the air traffic controller talks to the *pilot*, and no one else on the plane. You can have excuses or results. You can't have both. Ownership of a DRI eliminates excuses.

DO YOU PROCRASTINATE?

Get honest with yourself. Most procrastinators are in denial, as they explain away each item they push down the road. *Oh, I will do that later. This is much more important.* When they do not leave enough time to get somewhere, they blame it on the traffic instead of saying "I didn't leave early enough." Some people have had this problem for a long time, but to reach a significant *there*, they *must* overcome this habit.

There are many causes for procrastination—neurobiological, psychological, or even relational. Whatever the cause, you must deal with it. If it is neurobiological, address that with a physician or another appropriate expert. Behavioral interventions can be extremely helpful. If it's psychological, like a fear of failure or an inability to delay gratification, address those dynamics. Some of the other dynamics that can lead to procrastination include:

- Problems with emotional regulation
- Preference for immediate rewards over delayed ones
- Problems in executive functions
- Low confidence
- Perfectionism
- Aversion to difficult tasks
- Poor impulse control
- Self-doubt
- A bias towards present enjoyment over future good feelings of accomplishment
- Difficulty breaking large tasks into smaller, manageable steps
- Dopamine "addictions"
- Limiting thinking styles, such as negative self-talk
- Fear of being controlled by others and resisting to "feel free"

If you see yourself in one of these categories, make it a priority to get some help to end this destroyer of your desired future. Having treated or coached many procrastinators, I can tell you that it can be overcome. But in the beginning, you will need some outside structure and accountability to help you. Get it. In Chapters 7 and 8, we will address accountability as well, and that should help. But apart from the team or organizational accountability that we will be addressing, *please* tend to your own need for personal accountability and structure. Simply by having an enforceable deadline, the IRS can cure millions of procrastinators once a year, turning them into doers on April 14th. You might need to set some deadlines for yourself. Find them. My favorite? *If I don't get this done by Friday, I will write you a check for a painful amount.*

ARE YOU TOO OPTIMISTIC?

Sometimes, optimism bias is the best thing a leader can have. It drives you to believe it is possible, and to achieve it. I *love* that. It is one of the best traits a human can have, but we can be so optimistic that we make dangerous psychological errors. You can underestimate the time, costs, and risks that might come along the way, and find yourself in trouble and far off the path you intended. You can also assume that things will go well, a key trait of optimism, so you don't plan for problems, make contingencies, or realistically assess how hard things are actually going to be to get done. You are likely unable to see everything that must be done, or at least communicate it in a plan for those you work with. A plan takes care of this by grounding the necessary tasks, milestones, and deadlines in reality.

DO YOU SEE THE NEED FOR A LINEAR PROCESS?

In the beginning of the book, I said that everyone's problem is this: There is only one way to get from *here* to *there*. There are Five Essentials that must do what the human body does: vision, engage talent, strategy/plan, measurement/accountability, and fix/adapt. Your endeavor needs all five, no matter what your desired future is. But here is the problem we all share: No one person has all those strengths, at least not in equal measure. We tend to be good at a few of them, and weaker in the rest. But *your endeavor needs all of them to be strong.* So you must be like the air traffic controller, seeing it all and, even though you are not flying all the planes or doing all the functions, making sure that all five are present.

As I said, we tend to, until we wake up, build things and do things in our own image. If we are visionary, we will build a visionary company that is not good at planning because that stuff bores us. But our company, team, and individual endeavors need planning. The lesson of this book is: *Make sure it is all there*, even if that is not your strength area or tendency. Each one is important.

Check yourself and ask: *Do I see the need for a linear, outlined process and systems naturally? Do I tend to value them enough to give them priority as much as they need? Am I making sure they are all included in my company or team or my own projects?* If the answer to any of these is *no, not really*, then you probably have the reason why you haven't been able to reach your desired future before.

Think of it like this: If you do not like vegetables, when you go to the grocery store, your shopping cart probably won't be filled with everything your body needs. You will load it up with meaty proteins and tasty carbs. Think about your enterprise as a body, and make sure all the food groups, including planning, are part of your diet.

ARE YOU CONFLICT AVOIDANT?

A plan requires ownership, a reckoning with who is going to do what by when. In Chapter 7 on accountability, we address people to make sure that it is getting done. But sometimes, people who are conflict avoidant or have difficulty having hard conversations, struggle even in the planning stage. The plan has to state that Joey must do this by this time, and *own* it. The leader has to tell Joey, who might not like it, so instead they avoid the uncomfortable conversation with Joey, even though it is an important part of the plan. Leaders and doers face the difficulty of building a plan that might require them to tell other things they might not want to hear. Face that issue early, when the plan is being formed, so it does not come up and bite you later. The plan needs you to define the DRI, so do it.

Moving On

Your human body does not just keep standing there after getting a strategy and a plan. It begins to walk. *It's time to go!* This brings us to the next part of our model and what the human body can teach us about how to reach our desired futures. To avoid failure, tripping, or walking in the wrong direction, the brain asks the crucial question: *How will we know we are getting there and make sure that we do?* That is the question we will address in the next few chapters. Are you ready?

CHAPTER 7

Accountability: Are We Getting There?

Get quiet and undistracted for a moment. I want you to hear this phrase in your head for a minute before you continue reading. Hear it as if someone with power or leverage in your life is saying it. A boss, a peer, a loved one. Someone who really matters and can have meaningful consequences for you. Here we go: *"I am going to hold you accountable."*

Now that you have reflected, how does that phrase make you feel? Jumping for joy? Based on my experience asking that question of leaders, teams, and individuals for the past few decades, if you jumped for joy, you would be in a small minority. Most of the time, the responses are captured with words like: anxious, on edge, wary, scared, disheartened, judged, angry, annoyed, bristling, or stiffening up. These are all responses associated with higher-stress states, with bad chemicals being released that activate fight-or-flight readiness and the like. In short, many people hear *accountability* as a negative word—and for good reason. How many times have we seen a senator banging the table at a congressional hearing angrily and forcefully asserting, "SOMEONE will be held ACCOUNTABLE for this!!!" That's not what you want to wake up to. Even Judge Judy is nicer.

Accountability's cousin, feedback, has gotten a bad rap lately. As leadership expert Marcus Buckingham points out, most people don't like feedback, either. His research suggests one reason: The feedback often says more about the giver of the feedback—that person's biases and what they would have done in your situation—than it accurately reflects objective truths about behavior or performance.

Yet both accountability and feedback are important for personal and professional growth. Is there a better way? How can you turn your situation around, so that the next time you're asked to be accountable, you literally jump for joy?

Consider this scenario: You just boarded a flight from New York City to Los Angeles. You are sitting comfortably in your aisle seat, ready to settle into your great book or binge the show you downloaded on your laptop. *Ahhh.* All is good.

But you have a direct view into the cockpit, and you overhear the pilots' conversation. The copilot says, "Just got informed that the instruments are not working, so we won't have altitude, speed, or heading. And after we take off, the first 400 miles of communications with regional towers is down. They are telling me we can't go. What do you think?"

The captain answers, "Well, we have flown this route and this plane for a zillion flights. We know what we are doing. And you got that memo this morning from the CEO about no delays. We are losing customer loyalty by being late. If we wait till they fix this stuff, we might be here for hours. Let's just go."

Then you hear, "Good morning! We are closing the door and ready to take off. Weather reports this morning say it will be pretty bad in spots, so we will leave the seat belt sign on for a while until things are calmer. Sit back, relax, and enjoy your flight. We thank you for your business."

Now how are you feeling? "Is the Jetway door still open?" you ask yourself. "I'm getting out of here. They have no way of knowing where they are or where they are going!"

This example is unrealistic, and for a very good reason. In real life, commercial pilots have a very different view of accountability than we do. They see it as a *lifeline*, an absolute necessity for getting from here to there. They thrive on accountability and would never take off without their accountability checked, re-checked, and confirmed through a series of relationships with their copilot, instruments, air traffic control, and so on. Let's examine that.

Accountability Is Your Friend

I am sure that, like most people I have talked to, you have had some negative experiences with accountability. A few factors drive this. First, accountability is often used as a control mechanism by someone who is already unhappy with another person's performance in life or business. They want to get that person straightened out, whip them into shape, and put them on the course that they have determined is right. Their approach can be heavy handed and one-sided. I often use the term *police work* to describe this method. When do police hold you accountable? When they see you not performing as they or the law would like.

They hold you accountable *after* an infraction by taking the corrective action of writing you a ticket, or worse, if you have done something egregious. They might cuff you and take you to jail. In this way, accountability involves looking backward to enforce consequences and exact punishments.

While that aspect of accountability is important in certain contexts for obvious reasons, it functions only to contain mistakes or infractions. It serves to stop the bad stuff from continuing. Jail will contain a person so they cannot engage in some bad behavior, but it doesn't change what caused the problem in the first place. It's only a temporary fix. Said even better, it never prevents crime *before* it happens.

And that's how accountability often gets translated to the workplace and daily life as well—as a rearview mirror on performance that is tinged with shame, punishment, and other negative emotions.

The second reason accountability earns a bad reputation is how it's often delivered—with a scowl from a teacher or parent, with a dismissive shake of the head from a boss, or with a frown from a friend or spouse. The message is delivered harshly and with authoritarian or moralistic language that alienates the offender, making it hard for them to receive the content of the message and reducing their sense of psychological safety, which, as we've already discussed, is critical to engaging talent. As a kid, I did everything to avoid my dentist, who would shame me if I had a cavity. Guess what? I started to find excuses to avoid regular cleanings and checkups; a few crowns later, it was obvious (if only to me) that his treatment of me, hammering me with shaming accountability, wasn't going to work. It only led to more "fillings."

Another reason accountability is unpleasant has to do with cadence, how often it is meted out. Sometimes, too much time passes, and it can feel like a call for accountability comes out of the blue and without any warning. The hammer comes down, and you are being held accountable for things that you might not even know were perceived as problems. As mentioned earlier, this is what Ken Blanchard calls the seagull style of management, when a manager swoops in, makes a lot of noise, craps all over everything and everyone, and then flies away.

There's another reason why accountability often feels like a punishment, instead of an opportunity for growth or change. It occurs in a vacuum, without a foundation of trust—what I call the "soil of the relationship." Are the individuals planted in a soil of trust where input gets sown? Is the relationship safe and secure? If the answer is no, then accountability will be more complicated to create. Who feels good when you get a letter from the IRS? In my book *Trust*, I highlight the factors that drive trust, and two in particular load heavily on the tenor of the accountability relationship. First, does this person understand me and my context? By context, I mean things such as my background, what issues I may be dealing with, what kinds of interactions help me, hurt me, and improve me. Does the other person truly get me? Second, what is their intent and motive? Said another way: *Who is this for?* Accountability that seems to serve only the one holding someone accountable misses the mark. We do better in a relationship where we trust other people's motives and intentions. Air traffic control wants the plane to land safely: the best outcome for everyone, not just their own interests.

So, enough about why it can be unhelpful, toxic, get us off track, and even push things backward or at best cause them to stall. Let's solve that by looking at a healthier and more productive version of accountability.

TO ANSWER TO A TRUST

Historically, accountability comes from the word meaning "reckon or calculate," and it's used in a relationship where someone has been entrusted with something by someone else. One answers to a *relational* obligation where they have been entrusted as the steward over something, such as money, duty, responsibilities of an office, and so on. In feudal and early legal systems, when people were doing something on behalf of someone, they had to account for how that was going. It really is a relational word, grounded *in* the relationship and *for* the relationship, and its purpose was to make sure all was good, mutually reinforcing, and generative.

Take the pilot, for example. There is no way a pilot would take off without her measurement and accountability systems and relationships in place. She has been entrusted to protect passengers' lives and to avoid potential liabilities, such as damage to equipment or, worse, crashing into a neighborhood. It is a crucial exchange of trust between the individual pilot and the people and systems around her.

She takes that seriously, of course. She wants to accomplish her vision, get to LAX, and get there safely. She cares about the people, as well as the material consequences. Once again, we can see the five-part model at work in this example: The pilot has an unobstructed vision—get to LA, on time, without incident. Talent has been engaged, such as the ground crew, copilot, the cabin crew, traffic control, the FAA—everyone is doing their part. The pilot has a strategy and a plan that assigns accountability, including feedback loops in the form of checklists and other metrics to uphold that accountability. These are the tools that will make accountability possible to measure. And the plan gets very specific: We will fly on a 265-degree heading, at 35,000 feet, and 500 knots, in a specific amount of time. Now, with vision, talent, strategy, and plan in place, the pilot is ready to assume accountability for her part in the plan and to assign accountability to others for their parts.

Very soon, as the cadence demands in this instance, her accountability relationships begin measuring the first big question of accountability: *Is she doing what we agreed she would do*? She checks her instrument panel to be sure the settings match the plan. She's ready. She's accountable. All is a go.

Notice the difference here. Instead of accountability being negative, retroactive, or punitive, it is empowering and forward looking. Why? *Because it will help her to accomplish her vision!* Pure and simple. Accountability's purpose is *to make sure we get "there"! It ensures success.* Our pilot knows she will do better when she checks her accountability than if she were winging it without instruments. No pun intended.

And the cadence in this instance is quick. The loop between getting feedback and adjusting behavior (and her instrument panel) is tight, fast, and continuous. If, for some reason, she drifts down to 38,000 feet, she will get a signal from her instruments, her first level of accountability, that lets her know, "We agreed upon 40,000 feet and you are at 38,000." Instantly, she thinks, "Oops . . . heavier air will burn more fuel. We might get there late." She corrects, thanks to her accountability relationships and systems. (We will look at quickly fixing and adapting to accountability later.) Again, we see how the soil of trust plays an essential role: The pilot understands at a deep level that she is accountable not only to her employer but also to her passengers, her flight crew, and herself. This is not the superficial form of accountability we see dispensed all too often—a sort of "do this for that" exchange. Rather, it's a deeply felt, internalized feeling of ownership for results, for the *there* you're trying to achieve.

But she *loves* this accountability and would never take off without it. In fact, it is so important to her, and to her other accountability relationships, that she welcomes feedback. Imagine a pilot who got mad at the altimeter for telling her she was at the wrong altitude! What happens when she gets a call from the control tower: "United 21, heading 255, you are off your flight plan. Please correct." She doesn't balk, hide, or deflect. She probably says, "Thank you! I appreciate it . . . got a little distracted. Correcting now."

Here again, we see the dynamic between motivation and intention. When intentions and motivations are clear, when everyone is aligned around the goal—to get to LAX on time and without incident—accountability and its cousin feedback are a welcome gift.

Why? *Their purpose is to make sure she gets there. To make sure the vision is realized.* How? By having a plan that makes the strategy actionable and then helping her to get there by staying on plan.

It's worth noting, too, that the accountability exchange doesn't just involve correcting what's wrong. It entails helping fix what's wrong, to the extent it can be fixed. Here's another accountability conversation the pilot might have with the control tower:

"United 21, Las Vegas control. Your altitude is low . . . and inconsistent. Need correction to 40,000."

"This is United 21 . . . having trouble with the hydraulics . . . stand by . . ."

"Roger, standing by."

"Las Vegas tower . . . we are getting some glitchy response from the hydraulics. Are working on stabilizing altitude. Need assistance from company operations to figure this out."

"Roger. Connect to company frequency. We are standing by."

The point I'm making is that accountability relationships are in place to help, not to punish.

Accountability is not just a hypothetical thought experiment. It can have real-world, world-ending, and historical consequences, too. Remember when the United States reportedly almost went to nuclear war during the Cuban Missile Crisis? In 1962, the Soviet submarine B-59 lost communication with Moscow. Their accountability relationship was gone in an instant, and they were left to their own devices. Depth charges from our navy destroyers were signaling it to surface, but without the ability to check in with Moscow, and with no mechanisms to correct them, the Soviet crew believed that a war had started. All they could surmise was that we were now at war.

The Russian captain said to arm the nuke, adding that, "If we are going down, we will sink them all and not disgrace our navy." The absence of his accountability relationships, which were built on measurements and data from the real situation, put him in a vulnerable position to make a horrible decision. That is what the absence of measurement and accountability can do when we are essentially flying solo. We need to know where we are through measurements (data) and have an accountability relationship to help us. He had neither.

But thank God for accountability. Since this sub was armed

with a nuke, *it required extra accountability to launch*. Three officers were required to push the button. One of them, Vasili Arkhipov, said, "NO." He had the sub surface and await orders from Moscow. History could have changed without this life-saving aspect of accountability.

The same applies to far less dramatic and non-life-threatening situations that you might find yourself in as a leader, a manager, a team member, a spouse, a parent, or a friend. The purpose of creating accountability, grown in the soil of trust, is to help people get better at their endeavors, to help them abide by their commitments, and to live into their desired futures. It's not meant to figure out how to punish someone; it's meant to show how we can pitch in to help. It might be helpful to think of it this way: Accountability is more a series of questions than a declaration of duty. Accountability asks: *How are we doing? What happened to get us off track? What support do you need to succeed? How might we need to adjust the plan to get back on track?* And it asserts a clear and motivating intention: Let's figure it out together and see what we can do to help.

So, the next time you're about to ask someone to receive accountability, remember to put measurement and accountability in a positive light.

The Role of Measurement

When we don't have ways of knowing how we are doing and what we need to correct to get back on plan, bad things can happen. If a pilot, for example, loses instruments, and visuals are limited, they will experience spatial disorientation. They literally can't tell up from down. The inner ear gets confused (speaking of the body's system of measurement and accountability). Turns can feel funny and cause overcorrection and other miscues.

That's just a quick illustration of why accountability and measurement go hand in hand. One is lost without the other. If we don't have some way of knowing where we are with measurement, such as our altitude, speed, activity completion, sales, benchmarks, and so forth, then we don't have much to be able to be held accountable for. The accountability relationship has nothing, at least objectively, to talk about. Conversely, constantly measuring things without simultaneously tilling the soil of trust works no better and can, in fact, be harmful. I'm sure you know what I'm talking about: reports that no one reads, Zoom meetings where everyone is texting on their phone, deadlines that are fake, or performance reviews that parrot rote scripts.

Obviously, measurement for the sake of measurement is useless. *Measurement must be tied directly to the plan.* This is essential, as the plan is the structure that sets the pathway for the strategy to be implemented by the talent to accomplish the vision. When you begin walking, the human body has the vision of walking to *there*, and very soon after you get the vision, the brain begins calculating the rest of the chain of components in our model. Part of that is having an idea of exactly how the plan is supposed to go. Your brain calculates that it should take about ten steps, at about two or three feet each, at a certain rate in a certain direction. That is what the plan says you will do. Otherwise, you might start running or hopping across the room.

Then, as you begin to implement the plan, the body must be able to measure whether the plan is going off as, well, *planned.* So, it monitors the situation with an instrument panel of sorts to see that the limbs are moving at the correct speed and in the right direction. If course corrections are necessary, signals to the legs tell them to pick up the pace. Working together, the human body's systems, including the brain, are truly the most incredible design to get from here to there. Most of the time, it measures progress without our even being aware. The parasympathetic nervous system, for example, measures and corrects your heart rate, pupils, and other functions if they have suddenly gotten out of whack. That takes measurement. And if it can't fix it autonomically, only then does it get to greater awareness in your conscious brain, telling you: *We are measuring this, and there is a big issue here.* The brain has its own methods for fixing and adapting to inputs or, in my terms, measurements, something we will look at in the next chapter. But suffice it to say that the body never goes anywhere without its measurement and feedback systems in constant communication with each other. With some medical conditions, such as leprosy and congenital insensitivity to pain (CIP), the human body doesn't feel pain, which can result in harmful and dangerous consequences, such as not being aware of broken bones and not learning to avoid harmful stimuli such as flames or sharp knives. In these conditions, the body is missing a critical measurement system. Not to trivialize the seriousness of these conditions, but it's not unlike what I've seen in many organizations or in individual circumstances. If your business goal or personal path is not kitted out with a robust system of measurements and metrics to induce accountability, your vision is undoubtedly going to end up in trouble. You have real pain coming, and you don't even know it.

When your plan is off, the vision is in danger. Your body is already wired for accountability, but for personal growth and business success, you must deliberately create a system to identify what is "off plan" before it prevents you from reaching your goals.

WHAT DO WE MEASURE AND HOW?

A few years ago, I experienced three years of physical inactivity. I was mostly in a wheelchair, due to two total knee replacements and spine surgery, and scheduling delays due to Covid. I got fat, like way heavier than I had ever been. After sitting for three years with very little movement and unable to stand, I gained thirty pounds. For some reason, my injuries did not affect my ability to lift a fork to my mouth. Finally, I was up and around, and decided to get my act together.

I started with a strategy, a pretty standard one. I would eat less and move more. Watch my food and exercise. At the same time, I was really busy and traveling a lot, but I thought I was being diligent about eating less and moving more. I was pretty sure I was doing well. So, enter my only measurement system at the time: the scale.

After a few months of "being good," I was not losing weight. It made no sense. I was being good, or so it felt. And I was measuring with the scale. So, I wondered, "What is going on?" I had to ask myself, what would I tell someone else to do if they were not reaching a goal? Having worked for years with the model I'm describing in this book, I decided to apply it to my own predicament. I liked my vision and strategy, so that was all good. But I realized that my plan was pretty vague: *Eat less and move more.* I had to ask myself, "How is that actionable?" Sure, it had the who but lacked the what and when, the set of activities that I had to measure and hold myself accountable for. So, I repented and decided to make a detailed plan to make the same strategy work. I also got an app that would make the plan specific and measurable. It would measure exactly how much I ate and how much I moved, each day. Then it hit me—and this is the big point I want you to see about measurement: I had been measuring only a lagging indicator, not the leading indicators.

My measurement system, the scale, could only tell me what had already happened that week. It is like the scoreboard at the end of the Super Bowl. By the time I weighed myself, it was way too late to do anything about being behind. My weight was a lagging indicator of performance, in that it measured the *results of* what I'd done in the past, not what I was actually doing right now to lose weight. A leading indicator, on the other hand, is a measurement that signals *future outcomes.* Leading indicators are *measurements of the actions that are going to make the scale go down in the end.* The weigh-in is way, way too late. It doesn't tell me why I didn't get there, only that I didn't. And it doesn't tell me *how to make sure I will get there. It doesn't help me get there at all.*

So, I got on the app and plugged in the daily actions required to move the needle. I had to measure my eating activity, my exercise activity, and a few other things that the geniuses who programmed it had decided would make the strategy come to fruition. I then began to track my actual actions , which is what is most important.

Wow! My assumptions were *way off!* If I were a pilot headed to LA, there would be no question why I was continually landing in Mexico. My subjective monitoring of my eating was so out of whack compared to what was required that I found out I was not being as "good" as I thought, at least not to the level required to reach the goal. When I finally got specific and started measuring the *activities* that would have to occur according to a specific action-focused plan, I lost about twenty-five pounds. As I began to measure the *activities* that would make the plan work, according to the detailed plan, it worked.

The big mistake people make is monitoring results, which are the byproduct of specific actions and activities, not monitoring the activities themselves. They look at sales figures, for example. Say they have figured out they want a certain number of dollars in sales for a team each week. Great, you need to know how you are doing at the end of each week, but you also need to monitor whether your salespeople are taking the specific actions that the plan called for. In this instance, that might entail each salesperson making 100 calls each week, meeting with five prospective new clients every week, sending out three social media campaigns, and so forth. Don't just measure what you can see in the rearview mirror—sales dollars—monitor and measure the activities that will lead to the sales.

That's the lesson I was reminded of when I tried to lose weight. Weighing myself was necessary but not sufficient for my goal. My plan needed specific actions and a system of measurements for them—things like daily calorie intake and steps walked, for example—before the numbers on the scale would start to move downward.

Here are a few other examples of activities that could be monitored and measured to be sure a plan is taking hold:

- If you are building back a community after a disaster, monitor how many building permits your team issued that week.
- If you are creating online sales, how many e-mail campaigns were created and sent out that week?

- If you reduce employee turnover, how many one-on-one meetings occurred that week?
- If you are improving math grades, how many daily modules of flash cards did the child do that week?
- If you are trying to increase manufacturing speed, how many hours were the machines offline?
- If you are getting sober, how many meetings did you attend as your plan demands?
- If you want to become a singer-songwriter, how many hours a week are you practicing your guitar?
- If you are a competitive golfer, how many practice balls are you hitting a day focusing on a specific issue?

Consider how this might play out if you are creating unreasonable hospitality in the manner Guidara describes. Did each server report overheard conversations to the person on Guidara's team who would run out and make special things happen? How many ideas were acted upon? For customer satisfaction, did each floor worker greet the required number of walk-ins at the door, offering water or coffee, and asking how they could help? Actions like that are better than just telling the staff to go "be hospitable."

Even with Finley, accountability comes with measurement. Finley developed a urinary problem after spaying that requires medication. We have a calendar in the kitchen cupboard so that we can check off each day to confirm that we've given her a daily pill. That's a straightforward way to ensure that we do what we said we were going to do. Because of that, no soiled rugs. (And by the way, she needed to add some talent to her team to accomplish this ☺.)

Here's a familiar example of a measurement tool that doesn't go far enough. I'm sure you've seen one of those larger-than-life thermometers used by a charity, with the fundraising goal clearly marked at the tippy top. You can watch over time as the gap between today and the desired future narrows. But we all know that the thermometer is not going to fill itself. Only the effort of conducting the calls, meetings, and luncheons with patrons is going to do that. Measuring the right activities to make sure they happen is the secret sauce. The key: Define the specific activities that move the needle, that make a difference in the result. Then give them a time and person in the plan. Finally, measure them to make sure they are happening.

I've worked with a CEO who has grown a company from literally nothing to billions in revenue and multi-billions in valuation. One of his principal areas of focus is to identify what I named his *micro-drivers* of the business, *the little activities that drive results*. He makes sure his executive teams know them and focus on them like hawks. He has figured out that, for his strategy to work, he and his team have to drive towards these activities with extreme accountability. To close a sale, for example, he knows what elements the conversation with the customer must have, and he's trained his sales teams to keep awareness high by measuring those elements to produce the outcomes the strategy demands.

Root-Cause Analysis

So, we've built a relationship of accountability. We're measuring the right activities. But what happens when we come together to ask the first accountability question: *Did we do what we said we were going to do?*

Usually, at least a few of the numbers will not match up. There will be some sort of a gap between what we said we'd do and what we actually did. How you address that gap makes all the difference. Way too frequently, the gaping hole between what we said we'd do and what we actually did is met with a pep talk: *You have to do better! This week make sure you do five! Gotta step it up!* So, the person nods, gives a few excuses or reasons, but says, "I will. No problem, I will do better." And out they go with no clear direction on what needs to change. That's a big mistake. Fortunately, the fix isn't complicated, even if it does require a few more steps and a little more patience. How do you address it? You ask one crucial question: *Why not?*

This is called a root-cause analysis. It gets to the fundamental reason for the activities not getting done. And it is particularly important because if you don't fix the root cause, it will just keep happening. To do the same things expecting different results is not leadership. Or even good personal self-management. People who get from *here* to *there* resolve the problems that are keeping them from getting *there*, and if there are reasons why things are left undone, they get underneath the hood, tackle them, and work together to set things right by looking for those root causes.

What if the company's sales materials are too cumbersome to get through in five sales calls a day? What if the marketing group is slow in turning over leads so they can set up appointments? What if the leader has too many initiatives, some of which are almost impossible to execute and/or in conflict with each other? That is a leadership problem, not the person's failure, but it may be the root cause of failure all the same. In retail, what if the person on the sales floor must spend too much at the counter, closing the previous sale before meeting the next customer?

What if the cheeseburger is difficult to package, which slows down the drive-through window and backs up customers' cars?

The beauty of that question—*why not?*—is that it can help you quickly diagnose the essence of a performance gap. Drawing again on my own experience, by looking for root causes, I realized that my exercise metrics were off when I was traveling a lot for my work. I had to adjust my workout regimen to fit the weeks when I traveled, so I didn't have consecutive days of zero movement.

Root causes are everything, but notice this: You never can get to them if you haven't been measuring activities and holding accountability conversations with your teams (and yourself). If the body experiences pain in an ankle, the brain does not just send a message to walk better. If I am not hitting my word count, what might be the root cause preventing me from doing so? Could it be that I'm getting distracted working at home? Once I know this, I can rearrange writing times to occur during periods of silence, put up a "No Visitors" sign, rent/borrow a small workspace outside my home to enable complete focus. Whatever the root cause is, I can fix it.

The second big question: What if you find yourself in the opposite situation? If the measurements show that the planned actions were accomplished and done, that's great! Right? *Let's keep doing what we're doing. You are doing great getting the activities done!* But I am here to encourage you not to stop there. If the answer is yes, we did do what we said we were going to do, I encourage you to ask another question: Did we get the results we expected?

If the answer to that one is "Yes, we did! We got the results we expected," then, by all means keep doing it! Hire more people to do the same thing. Pour gas on anything that is working. Or at least, keep doing it again next week. Keep working the plan and getting closer to your goal.

But what if the answer is "No. We executed it perfectly but didn't get the results we expected. It didn't work." Then, you stop and revisit the strategy. Don't keep doing something that is not working.

You executed the strategy perfectly, according to Plan, and yet it is not working. That tells you, "I have a strategy problem," or at least an activity problem, in that the strategy might be good, but the activities are not the right ones to make your strategy work. For example, monitoring my food intake and exercise might be the right strategy, but maybe the exercise I am doing in the plan is insufficient. Maybe the strategy must be revisited. Dell won for years by executing low-cost computer components very well. But when hardware got commoditized and everyone could make computers cheaper, Dell had to pivot into services by formulating a new strategy for how to win. It is possible to execute a bad strategy well and continue to lose.

Great performers do not just charge ahead with more discipline. They have plans and measurements that reveal whether they have problems that need addressing or a wrong approach. But here is the key: Only by making a plan, measuring your adherence to the plan, holding yourself and others accountable, and asking those critical questions can problems be discovered. In addition to showing you the way and the how, the plan becomes a diagnostic tool.

It all makes sense, doesn't it? Create an accountability relationship. Monitor and measure the activities that align with the plan. How hard can it be? It turns out that, as logical as this process seems, there is often a monkey wrench thrown into the works. And that monkey wrench might be you. Let's look at some of the ways your thinking style and personality traits may throw off your best-laid plans and measures of progress.

What About You?

As in the other five essentials, measurement and accountability can be hampered or even missing, depending on our own issues. As Finley has shown us time and time again, we bark at the door because that's the way we're wired, at least until we can develop more self-awareness, diagnose some of the root causes that hamper us, and create new support structures to teach us that barking isn't the only way to get a treat.

As noted in Chapter 5, some of us are linear thinkers and some are more intuitive. I've seen a lot of intuitive thinkers struggle with measurement and accountability. They don't always appreciate the importance of the incremental steps and details that must be measured—they just want to see the P&L at the end of the quarter or the end of the year. When urged to ask "Why not?" when a target is missed, they may hear the answer as an excuse and miss the root cause. If this sounds like you, I hope you'll take to heart the message I've laid out here explaining why accountability done right is not only tough, but also kind.

Let's look at some of the other opportunities for personal growth that are available to you.

WHAT DOES THE WORD DO TO YOU?

Think back to the question I raised at the beginning of this chapter. When someone says to you, "I am going to hold you accountable," what kind of emotional response does that elicit in you? What kind of thoughts? Do you see it as a threat? A pressure? A controlling move? Do you feel fear? Resistance? Defensiveness? Do you brace yourself for a fight? Do you have the urge to hide? A myriad of responses are possible and understandable, depending on our personal experiences or personality style.

Get in touch with your own feelings and views on what accountability and being measured feels like to you. Maybe you like to play games when no one keeps score, kind of like some of my golfing friends who say, "Let's not keep score today. Let's just have fun." Measurement is keeping score. How does that make you feel? It might be more fun to play without a scorecard, but it also reduces your chances of getting better.

Once you become aware, find the resources to help you tamp down that response so you can move beyond it. That might take a bit of work, even therapy for some. But it is essential to develop a healthy relationship with accountability, for both yourselves and those around you—colleagues, bosses, direct reports, spouses, children, and even with the Finleys of the world.

Ask yourself and your team, "When has accountability and measurement been helpful to you? When has it been hurtful? What were the elements that were present when it was helpful versus when it wasn't?" Answers will be affected by your experiences in business, close relationships, or maybe even how you were parented. Those old voices don't go silent on their own without a little work, but you can choose new ways that reframe the past and help form a new way of doing it.

ARE YOU TOO NICE OR TOO TOUGH?

You can tell a lot about people by visiting a hospital's baby nursery, where all the newborns are lying there like swaddled burritos. Some are simply happy with the world, cooing and calm. Others are screaming and clenching their tiny little fists . . . future attorneys perhaps. Ready to litigate. My point being, we all have certain temperaments and past experiences that make us either try to keep things nice for ourselves and others, smoothing everything over, or we may already be fighters, quick to anger and quick to speak up.

I'm exaggerating to make a point and to encourage you to look at your default tendencies and style. If you are someone who always wants to keep things nice and harmonious—someone who would rather avoid conflict and confrontations—then it might help to think of measurement and accountability as something that is truly one of the kindest things you can do for someone else. You might ask yourself, "Am I doing myself or anyone a favor by not helping them see how they need to improve?" And if your default is to fight or dominate, then you might ask yourself, "How can I recast this exchange as a conversation among allies and collaborators, both of us acting with good intentions?" Fight-or-flight responses often reflect our temperaments, so be aware of how you perceive accountability.

WHAT ARE YOUR MICRO-DRIVERS OF SUCCESS?

Almost nothing is worse than feeling out of control. It is one of the bedrock elements of trauma. If we do not know exactly what drives the needle of results we are aiming for, even when things are going well, we will always be left wondering: *Why?* And when they go poorly, we will feel powerless. Some people keep stepping on the scale or looking at their bank account balance and still ask, "How did that happen?"

In the same way that a budget gives you control of your

finances, naming the actions that drive the results you seek gives you control of your desired future.

Whether it's counting reps in the gym, making 100 sales calls a week, sending seven positive comments to a kid or a spouse for every negative one—find the activities that serve your strategy and monitor them, and you'll feel more in control of your future.

One of the most important things you can do for yourself and for your business is to understand the 20 percent of activities that drive 80 percent of the results and focus on the 20 percent that actually move the needle the most. It will give you a much greater sense of knowing what you are doing and where you are headed, as well as a feeling of being in control of what is ultimately going to happen. We can only control what we can control, but we can't do that if we don't know what it is.

Moving On

Remember, it doesn't always have to be you and you alone. But it must be *somebody*. Do you have your "somebodies" in the right roles? Do you have an accountability relationship with them? It's all too easy, in the pursuit of a goal, to put the entire burden on yourself or to keep kicking the can down the road, not realizing that it doesn't always have to be you. That is often what teams are for. You do not have to do it all by yourself. Accountability and measurement systems help address that tendency, as they can become a team effort when everyone follows the plan. But it doesn't end there. Accountability also requires conversations with your "somebodies" in a productive cadence, a rhythm. In the next chapter, I'll say more.

CHAPTER 8

Accountability Conversations: What's the Right Structure and Cadence?

I was working with an executive team of a global manufacturing company, and they were struggling with the aftermath of a botched product launch. The issue was that they missed the launch date significantly, and when they were finally able to launch, the product disappointed a lot of customers, not because of its performance, but because it lacked features that the company had promised.

It turned out that the sales team, under pressure to meet their numbers, was pre-selling the product to customers a year before it would be available. When customers asked, "Can it do this?" many times they would say, "Sure, we can build that into it." The problem was that R & D and the engineers who had to make it work were not in those discussions, and when they found out they had to build those features in, they were only able to address a few of them. Then, the launch date had to be pushed back, which caused more disappointment among customers. This team certainly had a lot to work on.

We set up an executive team off-site to do a "postmortem" to find out where things went wrong. It was clear that mutual accountability for the plan and the process had gone awry, and that different pieces of the work and accountability had been siloed. As I worked with the players and the pieces to get them more integrated (which would have prevented this), I recommended that they build a system of *team* accountability that they could use on an ongoing basis. I will never forget our first discussion about it. I asked the team, "How do you like to be held accountable?"

One of the senior VPs said, "I'll go first. Whatever you must tell me, before you say whatever it is, just tell me I am not getting fired." We all laughed. She was very senior, a high performer, and loved by everyone. If anyone had reason to feel secure in their job, it was her. But her answer made me acutely aware of something we have mentioned. Most people have had experiences that have given them a negative outlook on accountability. Being measured and scrutinized can make any of us anxious, and for some, it is almost paralyzing. The last thing we want in a high-performance team, individual, or anyone who has to get something done is toxic fear.

In addressing this issue over the years, I have applied a dependable law of human psychology and behavior: *Structure reduces anxiety.* If we know what is coming, we will do better. And even better, if we can have input into what is coming, we feel more secure and have more clarity. One of the structures is the conversation itself—how you construct the conversation end to end can make all the difference, and applies to almost every situation—from parenting to working with teams to coaching CEOs running massive enterprises.

Step One: Make It Positive

Before you get into the nuts and bolts of accountability—the content of your feedback—open with a general discussion of accountability and their experience with it. Ask them, "When has it not gone well for you? What were the ingredients in that relationship?" When I'm working with teams at an off-site, I record their responses on a whiteboard. When you're meeting with a team or an individual, you don't necessarily have to write their responses down, but you can demonstrate that you're really listening by pausing, nodding, and not interrupting. Ask this with directness, but calmly and with kindness. Then flip the question and ask them about positive experiences they have had, and note those as well. You can use your team's input to help create the necessary psychological safety we've discussed in earlier chapters. This applies not just to how you communicate with the group, but also to how the group will communicate with each other. Ask them to agree to a behavioral covenant on how they will work together, ensuring accountability is perceived as a positive, not a threat. Have them agree to use the positive list and guard against the negative one. Those behaviors become their guide to accountability discussions.

That usually takes care of the negative view of accountability. It gets it on the table and addresses any land mines. You can do that with a one-to-one, a team, or even with your teenager.

Sometimes it might be helpful to have a purpose statement for your accountability conversations, such as: *We will hold each other accountable to what we have entrusted to each other, with the purpose of helping each other get there and accomplish our goals.* Get it positive. Who can argue with that?

Step Two: Mutually Agreed-Upon Expectations

Oh my gosh. If there was ever an 80–20 rule that was proven to be right, it might be that you could solve 80 percent of accountability issues if two things were true: We all know what the expectations are for each other, and we all have agreed to them. That avoids the "I didn't know you were wanting that! I would have done it differently from the outset!" conversations. Or the dreaded "You never told me that." And the endless ". . . but I thought" or "If I had known that, I would never have . . . " or "We have always . . ." or "Why didn't you tell me?" We have all been there.

When expectations are clear *and* mutually agreed upon by all parties, we are ready to go. State them clearly: *Everyone will have their budgets done and e-mailed to the entire team by June 1.* Then, we all sign on. If that date is a problem for someone, we can discuss it then, and not later. Get input, buy in, and come to an agreement.

In short, we are all expecting the *same things*.

Step Three: Define What *Done* Means

If you have had kids, especially middle schoolers or teenagers, you have had or heard this scene unfold: After dinner, everyone eventually goes off into their next evening activity, like homework, reading, watching something, or whatever they all do. They disperse from the kitchen. But Mom has told the kids, "Clean up the kitchen before you go do whatever you are going to do."

"Yes, Mom."

No worries, she thinks, and she goes off to the den to read her book. About an hour later, she wanders into the kitchen to make some tea. Then you hear the loud announcement resounding throughout the house:

"Kids! I told you to clean up the kitchen!" she yells.

"We did!" comes the reply from upstairs.

Then, her answer: "YOU CALL THIS CLEAN??? Get down here!"

The kids come downstairs, miffed to be called back into this task and resentful because they have already done their chore and are now being called back to the grind. Mom is standing there scowling, looking back and forth between them and the "unfinished" task.

Who's right? They both are. Who's happy? Neither party.

The reason is that each of them did what was required. Mom gave the order, and they cleaned the kitchen. But something was missing: the definition of *clean*.

This is a critical aspect of accountability: knowing when an expectation will have been met. One truth about human behavior is that we judge ourselves according to our intentions, while others judge us according to how our behavior stacks up to their expectations. After an argument, we might say, "I didn't mean to hurt you," meaning "It was not my intent." So we feel fine about what we did. But to the other person, the behavior was disappointing or even hurtful, laying fertile ground for conflict, feelings of disappointment, and even betrayal.

All of this could have been averted if what "meeting the expectation" meant had been clearly defined. "Budgets e-mailed by EOD May 31 with all categories and line items completed." "Mow the grass" might mean to run the lawn mower over every inch of lawn to a teenager, and to the parent, it means mow it, collect the debris, bag that, put it in the trash, and return all the tools to the garage. (For me, that calls up a memory of my father, who was a first sergeant in WWII.) Simply stated, you need to determine together how both parties will know when expectations have been met. Trust me ☺.

I know one woman who, after cleaning her kitchen and putting everything away like she wanted it done, took Polaroid pictures of the inside of the cabinets, counters, and shelves and taped them up on a pantry door with a note: "This is what I mean by clean."

Step Four: Define the Inspection Method and Cadence

Accountability conversations require what I call an *inspection*. It's a clunky word, so pick another if you want, but simply stated, it means that we have to know how we are going to check in on one another to see if everything has happened, and when that check-in is going to happen. Random audits are for law enforcement agencies or regulatory entities, not teammates.

Quarterly reviews or annual reviews are a lousy example. But at least you know when your work is going to be inspected and reviewed. If you're a manager, you've no doubt been told that these conversations should never come as a surprise to your direct reports because, if you have been having regular accountability discussions, everyone already knows how they are doing, and those meetings could be used in better and more forward-looking ways if all is going well.

The essential approach is to align the cadence of the inspection or accountability conversation with the needs of the plan. If certain benchmarks must be met or a critical path must unfold, we should have accountability conversations as the activities are being done, without allowing too much time to pass so that a problem goes unaddressed. In this way, the specifics of the plan drive the conversation, not the boss, and everyone is coming together, staring not at one another but at the standard enforced by the plan. We are all sitting in the same car looking at the same traffic light.

One of my favorite models and examples of this was Alan Mulally when he turned Ford around in the financial crisis of 2008. He had a weekly meeting at 7:00 a.m. every Thursday, and senior leaders were required to attend. No exceptions. He made that very clear. That is a cadence. It was very clear and *not* squishy. You had to be there, or else. And he meant it. The inspection method was that each leader had to present their data from the area for which they were accountable. Our aforementioned DRI. It was a "weekly business plan review." (Notice that it is tied to the plan.) They used color-coded scorecards to report in: green for on track, yellow for at risk, and red for off track. There was no hiding problems. This could only have happened because Mulally had established some psychological ground rules to *make it safe for everyone to use the time as a helpful experience, and not as a punitive one.* Problems were shared as opportunities for everyone to help with, and collaboration was encouraged. Respect for each other was expected, without blame or criticism. It was exactly what accountability is supposed to be: *a helpful way to make sure we get there.* He had ground rules for how they were expected to behave in these conversations.

Step Five: Does Anyone Want Something In-Between?

I was working with a CEO, and as part of the process, I interviewed her direct reports: "Tell me about Laura. What's it like to be on the other side of her?" The first person I asked said this: "She is the worst leader I have ever worked for. I feel like I don't talk to her enough, and I need more input. She is so removed that I don't often know what to do. It is like she ignores me."

As I listened, I was getting the picture of a detached, disengaged CEO. Uh-oh.

In my second interview, the VP said, "Oh my gosh. The best CEO I have ever worked for. Amazing is all I can say."

"Tell me about that. Why do you say that?" I asked.

He went on to list a few attributes, but then got serious. He said, "The thing that makes her so great is she gives me the space to go do things and does not have to talk to me all the time, she's not always in my hair like some bosses. I feel like she trusts me, and I am empowered to accomplish what we agreed to do. I feel so free and empowered."

What do these two distinctly different responses tell us? Both VPs had an internalized preference for what the right accountability cadence looked like. One was angry, and the other ecstatic. One wanted constant contact, and the other wanted to be left alone. Why?

As I hope I've made clear throughout this book, people are

different, and they work differently. Some are linear thinkers with high executive function. Others are creative and expansive and might need some direction. Some have high needs for inclusion, while others are emotionally fine on a desert island. *Just different*. What may feel like micromanaging to one may feel like encouragement to another.

While an established and regular cadence and structure are important, don't forget about the in-between time along the way. You might be able to tell one of your kids to do their homework and check with them in the morning as they head off to school, while your other child might need daily and maybe even hourly check-ins to see if they are okay or need some input. Adults are no different. *We differ.*

Once a cadence is set, have the conversation that asks: *What do you want me to do in between our accountability meetings? Do you want a mid-week "how is it going" text? Want me to drop by and take a look at how it is going? Want the freedom to come knock on my door?*

To discuss what someone needs in the in-between times is a good practice. It further creates clarity and permission, and can prevent people from feeling micromanaged or ignored. Hint: Your teenager will want less than your eight-year-old. And most wives want more "check-ins" than their husbands, in my observations.

Step Six: Define "What Happens Then?"

No one wants to walk into an accountability meeting, go over the agreed-upon expectations, come across a problem, and then immediately hear "Wait. You didn't get that done? You're fired."

By contrast, what if there have been several misses in a row, with many discussions, and the last discussion included a clear, last-chance warning that the next time, a firing would occur.

Those are the extremes, but part of healthy accountability is knowing that it is real and that it matters. That's never truer than with a pattern of misses or mistakes. You bring reality to the conversation when you define consequences and next steps. When you're clear about what happens now, you create the path for future steps. Here are some potential answers to the what-then question:

- We will do a deep dive and find out why, and see if the team or I can help with whatever issue we have uncovered, and then set a course to correct it.
- We will pair you up with a buddy from the team, and you guys will go solve it and report back in as to progress.
- We will get some outside help.
- Since this is continuing to happen, we will get you a coach. Or HR will be brought in. Or . . .
- You will be put on a standard of performance path, with gates and consequences.
- That activity will be given to someone else.
- Your role will have to change.
- You won't be able to use the car for a week.
- You won't go to the prom.
- If you aren't going to your anger-management meetings, I will be moving out and staying with my sister.
- You are going to rehab.
- You will have gained the opportunity to go be successful somewhere else.

As you can see, these are not punitive, but give clarity. In fact, most of them will be to take a deeper dive into the issue to clarify the question we discussed (*Why not?*) to do a root-cause analysis. It might be a leadership problem in that what has been assigned was unrealistic or under-resourced to begin with. And then remember, there are also positive what-thens:

- If we get all of this done, then we can close out this project and move on to buying another company.
- If you get this done, we are all going to the Lakers game.
- If you get this done, then I have a new role for you.
- If you get this done, there is a bonus headed your way.
- If you get this done, we can talk about my helping you get a car.
- If you get this done, you can have my job. "Really??"

Peers Are the Most Powerful

In many situations, the most powerful accountability structure is peer accountability. Remember, most times you are working on a strategy and a plan that is, by nature, interdependent. One person needs someone else to do their role so that they can do their own work as well. For example, did the sales team sell the features that are actually in the product? If not, we can't build the right one. (Remember that one?) Or is real estate on track to secure and build the new location so our team will be able to move in on our opening date? We depend on each other. The feeling of "someone needs me" is a powerful motivator, especially when team unity and trust are high. We don't want to let someone down or hurt them in any way if possible. (And if that doesn't matter to someone, you have a bigger problem.)

As with the structure Alan Mulally created, positive peer pressure and cross-functional help were essential ingredients. A recovery group works like this, too, as does a clinical therapy group. It is the group that holds members accountable much more than the therapist, who is there mostly to facilitate the process, to make sure peer accountability is happening. A good therapist will say, "I notice that she promised you guys she would break up with Joey, and it hasn't happened. What I am wondering is why aren't any of you saying anything?" The therapist is more interested in the peer accountability working than saying "Why didn't you break up with Joey?"

When peers make commitments to each other, research shows that the chances of adherence are higher in most situations. It is positively correlated with team commitment, trust, efficiency, identifying with the team, endpoint performance, sales, and so on. It also sidesteps authority issues and some of the initial feelings people might have about accountability. When this is done well, it is because the team itself is being held accountable for the outcomes. It changes the dynamic from "Just do your job" to "We must win." This approach also reinforces the importance of a shared vision and goal, and the power of engaging talent as a body. When the human body must walk across the room, and a foot is dragging, *the whole system chips in to help.* It is our problem to fix, the brain says, and everyone gets involved. A human body is a team, a group of many members, and as the Bible passage says, "The eye cannot say to the hand, 'I don't need you!' And the head cannot say to the feet, 'I don't need you!'" On the contrary, those parts of the body that seem to be weaker are indispensable. If one part suffers, every part suffers with it; if one part is honored, every part rejoices with it. (1 Corinthians 6:21,22,26)

Safety, not Toxic Fear

In 1996, the FAA and the airline industry were concerned, and rightly so. There was around one crash per 2,000,000 departures, and in that year, 350 people died. How do you fix that? By "measuring" them and then just telling airlines to "be safer next year"? No, you solve it in the exact methods we have been outlining here. And they did. For the next twelve years, 8 billion passengers were flown without a single crash. At the time the study ended, there was one fatality for every 120,000,000 departures. Pretty impressive, as the accident rate went from 2.5 fatal accidents per million departures in 1994 to 0.02 in 2007. That represents virtually eliminating fatal incidents for an entire decade, something that had never been accomplished before. The highways are nowhere near that safe. How did they do it?

The FAA supported an industry-wide accountability system that was based on *nonpunitive problem solving,* where people could bring their individual data, mistakes, and problems to the group without fear of retribution. The group included flight crews, maintenance workers, pilots, dispatchers, and so on. Near misses, errors, safety issues, and mistakes in equipment emerged. To solve these problems, the FAA and the industry used systematic error reporting that led to problem solving. *And they structured root-cause investigations to prevent it from happening again, as opposed to assigning blame.* Exactly what we have discussed. The point of accountability is to get to the vision, not to look back and do police work. The vision, no fatalities for a decade, was reached. They shifted the culture from blame to learning. Prevention, not punishment. They were looking forward instead of looking in the rearview mirror to assign blame or act like policemen writing tickets. It was a team approach, with engineers, pilots, and management all working together, driven by data—*things they measured.* It created a system of peer accountability, not just top-down authoritarian oversight.

But for this to happen, it had to be psychologically safe. Meaning, the absence of a culture of toxic fear, or irrational punishment and consequences. Sure, if someone planted a bomb in the fuel tank on an assembly line, they hopefully went to jail. But mistakes, not getting things done well or right, were not only safe to report, but they were also lauded for reporting them. Just like Mulally did when a manager reported their area was red, meaning the worst. He praised him for reporting it that way. Mulally encouraged that kind of honesty and transparency, and it changed the culture. That is what is meant by psychological safety. The message is: *We are not interested in punishing you, we are interested in solving the problem.*

Another of the best and simplest examples of what we are discussing here on structured accountability was the system that Atul Gawande reported in *The Checklist Manifesto*. Using examples from pilots to surgical teams, he talked about the power of checklist accountability, the specifics of the plan that drive the result.

The B-17 bomber crashed during a demonstration flight in 1935 in front of Air Corps officials. It had been heralded as the greatest plane coming online. What they found was that the plane was fine. It was not a mechanical or technical failure. The crash came from pilot error, because the plane's complexity *was just too much for the pilots to manage, and they got overwhelmed.* With four engines, multiple fuel mixtures, pitching mechanisms, and more, there was too much going on at once. Sound like your business or your life? It illustrates the principle that competency and smarts aren't enough. That is where the pilot's checklist was born, a remarkably simple accountability structure that is exactly what we have been outlining. The activities of the plan are presented as a handy checklist, which the pilots could review preflight to ensure (accountability) that the activities were all completed on time. What, who, by when. Then they could take off. After this method, the B-17 flew nearly 1.8 million miles without accidents, which led to its extensive use in WWII. This involved something like 13,000 planes. By the way, we won WWII. Vision accomplished.

Accountability systems such as this can be applied not only to airlines, but to manufacturing, parenting, and even surgical infections, which, as Gawande reveals, saw a 47 percent reduction in deaths and in major complications. All this came from simply asking "Did we do what we said we were going to do?"

That is not the only point here, though. There was no question around the world that the system worked, and hospitals adopted it to remarkable success. But some chose not to. The biggest failure was not from the failure of the system, but from some surgeons' attitudes that made speaking up psychologically unsafe for the team, because of blame, dismissive attitudes, reactivity, and other negative consequences. In other words, accountability breaks down when the atmosphere is not safe. Research shows that 81 percent of the teams saw problems, and 41 percent of them stayed silent when a surgeon created an unsafe atmosphere. (I don't want that surgeon operating on me!)

If you want short-lived compliance, be authoritarian. If you want improvement, make it safe for candid conversations. Some business leaders write this advice off as too soft or synonymous with laziness. That's not what I'm talking about. I'm talking about creating an environment where people can speak up, admit mistakes, and learn how to make things better. Make sure you are having the necessary discussions, developing accountability relationships, and building teams that work together with mutually agreed-upon expectations. Make it safe for everyone, and you will create a team able to confront reality and deal with it head-on. As Mulally said, "You can't manage a secret." But in the right conversation, when you find something is off plan, the atmosphere becomes one of "how can we help? Let's fix this and get *there*." It is not soft at all. No one gets off the hook and problems are certainly being addressed in a helpful way.

What About You?

Are you positive or punitive? We all have psychological structures in our heads that notice and evaluate negative reality. A mistake, problem, or annoyance. We need those, or we would never know something is wrong or off-kilter. That is the awareness aspect of evaluating our work, selves, others, and the environment. Or your body telling you that you have an infection. That is good.

But those evaluations are also tied to emotional responses or reactions, memories, and a host of other networks in our brains, minds, and souls. Some are helpful and some are not. We need to be aware of and notice in real time the responses that are not helpful. And, until we do, we are apt to respond to mistakes with an emotional reaction that may not be particularly helpful and may certainly be harmful.

So, look at your internal response when faced with negative occurrences. Do your responses match the actual danger of what is occurring? Do you need a moment to calm yourself before responding? And how do others see you? You might ask your team or others how they feel when you hold them accountable for something, as these reactions are often out of our awareness. Someone can not intend to come across as toxic, but does so all the same. Get some feedback, become aware, and work on it.

Do You Feel Like You Have Lost Control?

As I've noted, setting expectations requires mutual agreement. People respond better when they have buy-in. Does this mean that people under your supervision or answerable to a team can just say, "No . . . I am not doing that"? Not if they want to be in that position very long!

Sometimes, when the resistant person doesn't agree with your expectations, you may need to hear their "why" first. Most of the time, with all things being equal, the best route is expectations being mutually agreed upon. Sometimes, though, that doesn't happen. But even when you can't reach a mutual agreement on an expectation, and you must require it anyway, just make sure the individual knows that you understand their reasoning. Then you can take your stand and say they have to do it anyway. If you have adequately heard them, you are more likely to be able to move them to a stance on which they can say, "I disagree, but will fully commit." That is the agreement you must reach, or you will continue to face resistance, or something worse later.

But let's face it: Not all decisions or expectations are unanimous. Bosses exist; teams exist that might be going in a direction different from the one you'd prefer. Ever been a parent? But ultimately, a person must commit to accountability and authority. That's an important milestone too, as it clarifies whether the accountability relationship should continue or whether it might be time to part ways. With a healthy dose of psychological safety, even those conversations can be conducted with kindness and good intentions.

Do you tend to pressure people into compliance or are you able to hear them out first when disagreement arises? If your team, your company, your family, or your community has never discussed psychological safety and what makes it work for everyone, then you would do well to bring that up and drive that effort. Check yourself and check your culture to see what part you can play in driving that value to the top.

Can You Enforce "Done"?

We talked about how we must make sure the expectation is *fully* met. This is the road to excellence. Sometimes, however, people feel like they are being nitpicky to see something 80 percent done and require the other person to do more to fully reach the definition of *done*. They have a tough time saying, "That's progress, but it's not finished yet. I need you to go get it to the finish line." Remember, they *have* agreed to that.

Some feel bad or guilty after making such a demand. But in

some cases, like whether an airplane can fly, excellence matters. Check yourself to see if you are just too soft sometimes and lack the stomach to hold people to their commitments.

Are you a 90 percent person? My dad had a saying, "Good enough for who it's for. Let's go." He usually meant good enough for us. I would feel relieved. But when he would say that it was "good enough," it actually was "good enough." He didn't waver. We moved on. Yet, I assure you, as a former sergeant, he had no problem making it perfectly clear to me when it was *not good enough*. He had no problem telling me to go back and finish it. (*You call that grass "mowed"?*) You might have to develop a little tenacity to step into that place in your own tasks, and model what *done* looks like for others. Excellence is contagious, and it begins with us and our ability to set limits on what excellence requires.

Does Avoidance or Micromanaging Throw Your Cadence Out of Whack?

Remember the importance of the cadence, how frequently the inspections and check-ins are needed. The antibiotic must be taken on a scheduled regimen for a specific reason. You need the next pill before the earlier one loses its punch. Go too long, and you are basically starting over.

If you are avoidant, you might be prone to allowing big gaps between the conversations and the check-ins. Or, if you are a little anxiety prone about whether someone is performing up to snuff, you might impulsively jump in and be really driving them crazy. If you have agreed to a working cadence of accountability or rhythm, then stick to it. Monitor your internal world if you have resistance to following through, or resistance to waiting until it is time to regroup. And make sure it is the right dosage. Not too often, or not often enough.

How Do You Feel About Enforcing Consequences?

Boundaries are not boundaries without consequences. Said another way, you will get what you tolerate. Sometimes, the problem is that someone has said that a certain "what happens when . . ." will be enforced, but then when it happens, they find it difficult to enforce that next step, which is sometimes a consequence. This is the parent who says, "You will not be allowed to play if you don't do your homework first." Later, when the kid cries about not being able to play, the parent folds with just a weak lecture or meaningless threat for "next time you do this, then . . ." The kid is deaf to that promise, since the last one meant nothing.

Check your gut. What does it feel like to know you have to follow through with some kind of consequence to an accountability expectation? Are you afraid? Does it feel mean? Are you afraid of not being liked? Numerous fears may drive this feeling, but expectations are meaningless if not enforced. Sticking to boundaries builds respect, for you and for reality.

Have You Developed an Accountability Culture?

This is important. When everyone values accountability, it really ups the game, but that requires some work to build the soil, the culture. Have you done that?

I remember when I was in graduate school, living with four other guys in one house. We were all going to school and working, and let's just say, keeping a clean kitchen was not the top priority for anyone. Dishes would stay in the sink, pots on the counter—it was a mess. We were always yelling at each other to clean up after ourselves.

Finally, we entered an accountability program with everyone agreeing to its terms and its consequences. We were each designated an area for our dirty dishes. Midnight was the deadline to have all your day's dishes done. If anyone's section still had dirties after midnight, then anyone else was free to wash them, and the offender owed that person twenty bucks. In graduate school way back then, $20 was a fortune for any of us.

The most amazing thing happened. Almost *every* night, at midnight, the kitchen looked great. At various times, however, someone would miss a day, leaving some dirties in their area for whatever reason. It became a regular thing for all of us to gather around at 11:55 each night to pounce on the stack of dirty dishes. Cleaning up had morphed from a painful task to sport hunting. And it got hilarious to see whether the offender would come rushing through the front door at 11:59, just in time to wash their dishes, or whether they'd arrive at 12:01 to see someone else washing their dirty utensils and have to pay up. "What happens when," meaning the *consequences*, make accountability real.

It's silly, I know, compared to some things you have to deal with. But the principle is that when everyone becomes an accountability champion, and everyone shares that value, and believes in the reality of the consequences, it gets better. It can even be fun and energizing. (Unless someone gets fired, and that is not fun, but it does often prove energizing in a different way. It shows that the culture or performance is real.)

Moving On

So, hopefully by now you are getting the model and seeing how it fits together. Vision, engaging talent, strategy/plan, measurement/accountability . . . so far. But notice where that leaves us. We have just had some accountability discussions, and hopefully everything is green, in Mulally's language. But . . . what if it isn't all green, or there are issues? What if a problem has surfaced?

How long will you let that known problem remain in place and do its damage?

That is the subject of the last essential element on the path to your desired future, "Fix and Adapt." Let's look at that one now.

CHAPTER 9

Fix and Adapt: Avoid Patterns, Not Problems

We all know the feeling. Think New Year's resolution. You have dedicated yourself to something—a new project, working out, a new direction in life, an early morning quiet time, or whatever. This requires you to get up earlier than you are used to. Like, more than once. Maybe not every day, but several days a week. That is the plan.

You float along all right due to the initial momentum and excitement about the new direction you have taken, but at some point, you hit the well-known motivation dip. The alarm goes off, and you just don't feel like it. Even though you didn't feel like it on other mornings, and you still did it, this time you just decide, "Gonna skip it today. Too tired." You roll over and go back to sleep. No worries, you promise yourself, you will do it right tomorrow, so it's not a problem. And many times, you do. You know what? No big deal. You have not killed your program by missing one morning any more than you have ruined your healthy eating with the occasional cheeseburger. In fact, research shows that a slip or skip is normal and does not necessarily derail anyone (other than the way it can derail an alcoholic or other addict) from achieving their goals.

But if that second morning comes and you do it again? *Chances are, your program might be headed for the failure bin.* Not for certain, if you take some remedial actions, but there is a significant decline in momentum, habit formation, and probable success. If it happens a third time? Good luck. Without some kind of intervention, you might as well never have even tried. Research continually reveals this finding: that once we allow a problem to persist, or permit some failure to do "what we said we were going to do," we might as well see it as concrete drying. The problem becomes hard and fixed.

Why is this? There are myriad reasons, but if you're using the lessons I've laid out in previous chapters, you already know why accountability is so important: It not only reveals a problem, but it might also even prevent something from becoming a problem in the first place. Let me be clear about problems: *It is not a problem to have problems*—that is what life is about. The issue is when we don't address the problem. That's why we need accountability and a method for adapting to reality and fixing issues to prevent concrete from forming.

Performance is all about solving problems and resolving obstacles. When you are walking across the room and start slowing down, distracted by someone in the crowd, you have a problem. You didn't do what you said you were going to do. No big deal. But your brain's accountability and measurement systems alert you that you are standing in one spot too long, and you get back on track before the new, slower walking speed becomes your "new normal," a phrase that we should learn to fear. *The human body does not easily allow a "new normal." It fixes problems quickly.*

And what happens to problems that don't get fixed? They become something much worse. They become *patterns*.

Not a Problem

When problems are not solved and are allowed to recur, they become *patterns*, or "the way we do things." And here is the danger: Patterns get wired into structures of behavior. Even neurologically. Like DNA, they mutate, becoming new ways of doing things. Suddenly, your plan has morphed into something you didn't intend. Unknowingly, you've fallen into a new pattern, a new plan, and a new identity. Recall the example I mentioned previously—the company that missed a product launch. If they miss another one, they are no longer "the company that missed a product launch." They have now become "the company that misses product launches." That is what they now do, repeatedly. It is no longer a problem; it is an entrenched pattern. It is the "new normal" for them. Similarly, we are no longer the person who missed Tuesday's workout. We become the person who doesn't get up and work out, doesn't watch what we eat, doesn't make the required number of sales calls to improve revenues, doesn't do the planned safety checks in the manufacturing process, doesn't connect with our loved ones, which means we've become the company whose planes now fall out of the air. We become our patterns.

Accountability measurements reveal issues and problems, hopefully not just when a deadline is missed, but much before that. But *accountability does not fix things. It only reveals what is happening (or not happening). It is up to us to "fix and adapt."* And here is the kicker: *Waiting usually ensures time for the pattern to take root and go deeper.*

Recently, my wife and I noticed that our driveway was getting a line of dirt running across it after some prolonged heavy rains. "Where is that coming from?" we asked.

Upon examination, we traced it back and discovered that the drainage system wasn't able to handle the heavy rains, so water was running over and flowing down a slope. If it had happened just one day, it would not have been a problem. But a repeated pattern had now formed a *structure*. Over a series of days, that steady stream of water had carved a makeshift canal into the dirt, a new path for the water to flow down the hill, creating its own new drainage system. Fortunately, we addressed the problem before we ended up with a lake in our front yard. Neurological patterns get formed in much the same way.

This is why great performers do not allow problems to become patterns. Patterns become the way you do things, and you do not want those patterns to be formed from systems and structures—behaviors, habits, processes, thinking styles—that are malfunctioning. It's a lot easier to remove a bad seed from a garden than to cut down the weed. Nip it in the bud.

The Immune System

Once again, we can turn to the human body for a useful model. Without going into too much detail, you can think of the body's immune system as an extraordinary "fix and adapt" system that deploys measurement and accountability mechanisms to keep you healthy and defend against "invaders" (aka bad patterns).

In the body's immune system, prevention mechanisms meet potential problems, bacteria, for example. First, skin and mucous membranes trap the bacteria in the nose, lungs, and GI tract, for example. In the respiratory tract, cilia sweep it out of the airways. These first-line systems try to prevent the bacteria from entering your body. But stuff happens. If the pathogen does make it through these early gatekeepers, the "fix it" system moves back into action, unleashing more saliva to tear it apart, tears to flush it out, stomach acid to destroy it, digestive enzymes to break it down, and acidic urine to chemically and mechanically flush it out. If that doesn't work, the immune system ups the ante, triggering T-cells to release antibodies that target the issue. If those fail, other resources activate to further take on the challenge.

The point I'm trying to make with this whirlwind trip through the miracle of our immune system is that values and norms are the first-line tools for preventing bad patterns from emerging; they are akin to the skin and mucous membranes of the body's immune system. They determine what kind of behavior and performance you are going to allow to be part of your life or your business. For instance, if your desired future is to be a healthy person, then one of your norms might be to put your workout clothes out the night before so they're ready to go. Another one might be to only stock your fridge with fresh fruits and vegetables. If your professional goal is to launch a new product on time, on budget, and with all the features you've told customers they can expect, you need to embrace values, norms, and structures that, first and foremost, prevent bad patterns from taking root. For example, the norm of "we inform all departments that will be affected by what we are going to do."

In a high-functioning accountability system, the flow looks like this: first, prevent it; second, detect the problem once you have it; third, respond to it quickly; and finally, eliminate it. If that doesn't work, bring in a more targeted response to make sure it really gets done. But above all, do not allow it to continue.

The First-Line Response

I was conducting an off-site with a leading tech company, and one of the regional leaders was talking about their accountability meetings. She revealed that when an issue surfaced and two people were connected to it, each would come to her individually, offering their own perspective. Sometimes, they blamed each other, but mainly, they wanted her help to solve it. She said, "I am too involved in problem solving for my people. How can I not do that?"

I told the group a story about my daughters when they were younger. They would come running to me and Olivia would say, "Lucy did x or y." And then Lucy would say "But, Olivia did z first," and launch a counter accusation. This was becoming a pattern, happening more than once or twice.

One day, I interrupted them and said, "Okay, girls, you have a dispute and you are bringing it to what I am going to call, from this day on, Daddy Court. Daddy Court is when you bring your complaints about the other one to me and argue your case. In Daddy Court, I am the judge, and I will decide who is right and who is wrong. And that decision will stand.

"But, here is the way it works: *Loser pays*," I continued.

"What does that mean?" they asked.

"Well, there are court fees. Daddy Court is not cheap, the judge's time is expensive, and we are using valuable space in our house to hold court. So, when you bring a case to me, I will declare a winner and the other one, the loser, will pay the court fees," I explained.

"What are those?" they asked as I detected a bit of growing concern about this new immune function.

"Depends on how long the trial lasts," I said. "But it could cost you your skateboard, or an American Girl doll outfit . . . maybe even your *bike* if the trial takes too much time. Depends. There are short trials and more difficult ones. I just must get paid for court costs, that's all."

They looked at each other and said, "That's okay . . . we will go figure it out." And they left.

In a similar fashion, I advised the tech executive to have a conversation with her two direct reports, emphasizing that she wants them to solve these issues with peer-to-peer fixes. Relating the analogy of the human body's immune system, I told her, "You are like a T-cell-level response. You are a big deal. They are the saliva or stomach acid level and should fix this without your involvement or even knowing about it."

She smiled and said, "I like this." Of course she did. She would rather focus on bigger issues than the ones people should own themselves.

I remember an off-site with another medical industry company that suddenly found out the FDA was doing a random spot visit in the next day or two. The risk management and compliance VP wanted everything to stop and the factory shut down for a day to prepare, as that was their role: compliance. But the sales group went ballistic because of what that pause in cranking out product would do to their promised delivery times to customers, not to mention what it would do to their plan, which was to generate revenue and guarantee customer satisfaction. "We can't shut everything down!" they protested.

They both came running to the CEO, and the off-site was totally derailed. They were trying to enter Daddy Court. The CEO immediately responded as a great leader should. He told them, "We are going to take a one-hour break. I want you two to go to another room and find me a solution where the inspection can be prepared for, and we can also meet the delivery dates." In an hour, they had it solved.

Many times, what accountability can and should lead to is for the problem to be solved at the level closest to the action, by the right people closest to the action. As a leader, you don't want to, nor can you, solve every problem; that's why healthy norms and values—put in place before a problem arises—matter. Even better is a norm that encourages team members to ask, "*What other preliminary fix conversations can happen before the rest of us have to get involved?*" Develop a norm where problems are fixed at the "saliva level" without having to get to a higher-level immune response. If that becomes a normal immune function, happening at the cubicle level, the head (aka the CEO) never even knows a threat of infection occurred. With a good immune system, fixing problems early and quickly, at the lowest level, becomes the norm.

One last example of what quick looks like: I am a lifelong boater and have had many boats, from small to large. The first one I ever had that was large enough to have complicated systems surprised me on my first trip, heading from Marina del

Ray, CA, to Newport Beach, a trip of about fifty nautical miles. I went down to the master stateroom to get a sweater. I had been on the flybridge with the yacht broker who had walked me through the purchase.

When I was down there, I heard a noise that would hum, click, be quiet, begin to hum again, click, and then be quiet. Soon, the humming would start back up. Immediately, I thought there was a problem I was hearing through the wall of the engine room. This intermittent noise that would start and stop and then start again sounded like something was really wrong. I ran up to the bridge to tell the broker, since he was the expert on the systems of the boat, that something was broken and that I was worried it might blow up in the engine room. I told him I could hear it through the wall. Not loud, but I could hear something.

He asked me to describe it, and apparently, the way I did was not helpful. He said, "Show me," and we hustled down to the stateroom. It was quiet. He said, "I don't hear anything."

"I swear I heard it," I said. "Something isn't right."

Just then it happened again. Hum, click, quiet . . .

"There is it!" I exclaimed. "What's wrong?"

He laughed. "That's the autopilot," he said. "I set it a little while ago, and it is driving the boat on our heading to Newport."

"Ohhhh . . ." I said, a tad embarrassed that I hadn't known about this feature. I had never had an autopilot on my previous smaller boats.

"So, why is it making that noise?" I asked.

"Well, I set the heading, and the boat goes on that heading until the nav system senses that the wind, or the seas, have moved us off of the heading a few degrees. When it determines that, it immediately corrects the heading through the automatic steering system and gets us back to the exact heading we need to be on," he explained. "It corrects the mistake in the direction we are headed."

"Wow," I said. "It seems to be almost constantly working. Hum, click, then gets quiet and then it does it again . . . seemingly pretty quickly."

"Correct," he said. "At least the way I have it set right now. We are in some big swells, and the boat can get hit hard and quickly be aimed a few degrees off. *If we continued in that direction very long, we would end up somewhere other than Newport Beach!* It has to constantly monitor and quickly correct the mistakes to keep us on track. If it waited a long time to correct, we would lose time and fuel or worse. So, considering the seas today, I set it for quick, pretty quick correction sensitivity."

What an incredible illustration of the measurement and accountability system I'm suggesting you adopt. It offers all the elements of a successful accountability program: detection, response, and elimination. *Hum, click, quiet.* Your accountability system needs to work constantly and quickly to clear problems from your path. An airliner's autopilot will make hundreds of thousands of corrections to the different systems in a normal coast-to-coast flight. Let's look at some other quick-fix methods that can help, in addition to others I've previously described, such as root-cause analysis (see Chapter 7).

Hypothesis Testing

An old model that many find helpful was developed by Walter Shewart and Edward Deming, and began being taught back in the 1950s. It says to "plan-do-check-act." This is an iterative approach that can help you test whether your potential fix will solve your problem. It works like this: Come up with a change, test it through experimentation, and see if it works.

Some critics of this approach claim it can be too rigid and may limit innovation or be misapplied in some way. But the basic idea is worthwhile: find the problem, understand it before acting, get the right voices to address it, act on data, make small bets first, remeasure, and see how it is going.

Maybe Fix Me First?

I often refer to the old story about the dog-food company whose sales were flat. The founder called in everyone and was livid. "Fire the advertising company!" he screamed. "We need better marketing!"

So, they did. The next sales cycle, the numbers were still bad. He repeated, "Fire the new one and get another one! And get a different dog for the picture on the bag!"

And they did, and sales were still bad. This continued for another few quarters. Hiring and firing ad and marketing agencies. Finally, at the next meeting, he was scolding everyone about sales again, and a man in the last row raised his hand.

"What, Jones?" the founder angrily asked.

"Sir . . ." Squeamish Jones replied, "the dogs don't like it."

Ouch. It was the founder's recipe.

Sometimes, when we are in a position to hold someone else accountable, like this boss, we may overlook or discount the role we play in hindering their progress. As my dog trainer taught me, it's usually not the dog. It's the owners.

One of my favorite principles in life is one that Jesus taught. He said that instead of judging others, we should "get the log out of our own eye first, before trying to remove the speck out of someone else's eye." He added, "Then you can see clearly to remove the speck out of their eye." We often cannot accurately evaluate another person's issue if we have not dealt with our own contribution to the matter at hand. Awareness of self is its own kind of accountability.

Role Confusion

A related issue stems from ambiguity about who does what. Peter Drucker reminds us that this is the most vital role of a leader. Take a moment to see if there is confusion about the ownership of a task. Sometimes two people have their hands on a steering wheel, and that is not good; other times, no one does, thinking someone else is doing it. Great leaders ensure that ownership and responsibility are known to all, but then you also must ensure that the levers needed for that role are available for them to pull. Are you addressing role confusion in your actions? Are you giving people what they need to succeed?

- Did you give them the training they need?
- Do they have the right tools to get it done?
- Do they have the money to get it done?
- Do they have the people they need to get it done?
- Do they have the systems or processes needed?
- Do they have your political support and cultural cover or championing?
- Is the plan clear with proper ownership assigned?

- Are you checking in along the way as discussed, or AWOL?
- Is your tone or attitude contributing something toxic to high performance?
- Have you made what is expected clear?
- Have you given competing tasks or priorities, or have you communicated them as if they are all equal?

It is easy to point fingers and assign blame to the one who is not getting it done. But sometimes we might be part of the reason they are not meeting the expectation, and then we become part of the answer as well. I remember in one of my companies when a particular department told me they were understaffed to meet my expectations. I thought they were wrong. Then the manager came to me with data showing that the ratio of staff allocated to him was way out of whack with other departments, even smaller ones with way less revenue expectations. Ouch again. It was on me.

The Pygmalion Effect

The Pygmalion effect is a psychological reality where higher expectations lead to improved performance. In a famous study by Robert Rosenthal and Lenore Jacobson, elementary school teachers were told that certain students were expected to show more growth. In reality, those students were chosen randomly, meaning there was no reason to expect they would be superstars.

When the teachers had those expectations of those students, those students showed greater improvement than the others, in both IQ scores and performance. So, when you are trying to fix performance issues, and grow people where problems have arisen, having high expectations for them to be able to fix and adapt can have a powerful effect. You will tend to give them the attention, support, and guidance they need, give better feedback, and create a warmer climate, and that can have powerful effects. Keep that in mind as you look at the problem person. They might surprise you, based on what *you* do.

It May Be Them, Not You

I've made the case throughout this book that many problems happen due to a lack of good systems and structures, but sometimes we look into the issue, remove all the obstacles, and find out that it really *is* that someone is to blame. Meaning, this person has everything they need, but they still aren't getting it done. They are the weak link.

There are several reasons for that to occur . . . lack of work ethic, lack of buy-in, low personal standards, lack of skills, character issues, lack of knowledge, and so on. And if nonperformance is an issue, there are well-known paths to address that, from coaching to training to others. Develop them if that will do the trick. All good. And we owe it to people to try to help them succeed before showing them the door. But after you have done all that you can do, sometimes it is time for a necessary ending, as I wrote about in the book by that name. It's sad, but sometimes it's a necessary truth. That does not always mean they have to go away.

I was at an off-site recently with a company working on trust. I asked each VP to share an example of when they were able to turn a situation with a leader around from failure to success, by using the principles from my last book, *Trust*, which the company had adopted as an organization-wide training program. Briefly, I reviewed the five factors that help determine whether you can trust someone: understanding, motive, ability, character, and track record. All five must be present for a relationship to have a durable foundation of trust.

One of the executives beamed when she said, "I have a great example." She described a situation where one of her direct reports, a leader who was getting horrible marks from people he supervised. Despite this executive's numerous accountability conversations with the low performer to remedy the situation, his performance was persistently poor. The biggest issue was the leader's micro-managing of projects, slowing them down and getting in everyone's way without adding value. He was *soooo* detail oriented that he would inspect and turn over every speck of dust, so that timelines were blown. People were unhappy, no matter how many attempts the executive made to "fix" him. Finally, something dawned on the executive: "I realized that this guy is horrible with people. Horrible. He drives them nuts. He is so overinvested in details that he can't see the big picture.

"Then I had another thought," she continued. *"Why in the world do I have him leading people when his skill is with data and details?"* The executive went on to explain that she'd found a different role for him, one that requires the specific abilities he has. Now he is thriving, generating digestible reports from mountains of details that help the rest of the team quickly review otherwise complicated facts and figures. Now the same people who hated him when he was managing them are beating his door down for analysis and actionable tactics. As the executive put it: "He has gone from village villain to hero! And he is managing no one! Everyone is happy, and the results are great." By using the trust model, which begins with gaining a deep understanding of the other, a solution was found. There was a necessary ending to the problem, but in this case, not for the person.

Not all situations have a happy ending, though. Sometimes the fix is not the person being in the wrong seat on the bus but being on the bus at all. Sometimes, the person is not going to get better, and it is time for them to go. Most of us don't want to make decisions that cause pain for people, but sometimes we must. That's one of the values and norms that help create and reinforce a culture of accountability, a culture that *prevents* problems from becoming hard-to-break patterns that take root in the organization, or even in a family or relationship.

Figure Out Who You Are Talking To

Here is a framework that might help you get to the essence of whether you are dealing with a fixable problem with a person or a dangerous pattern: *Figure out who you are talking to.* Let me explain. As I said in *Necessary Endings*, psychiatry, psychology, theology, human resources, and other systems that deal with human behavior and performance have all agreed that all people are not alike, and at least their behavior can be put into categories. Psychiatry historically called people with issues but who are ready to listen and respond to help "neurotics," as they have the ability to see and own their problems. They feel bad about it and want to do better. We can try to work with them. We can always try to fix issues with each other if each person is willing to listen and change. But the second category of people is not so easy to deal with. In psychology, they are referred to as people with character disorders, and are the ones who will not welcome feedback or even agree that they have a problem. No matter how much you try to coach them or get them help, they blame either you or someone else, but the problem is never them, in their eyes. The third category, which psychiatry refers to with labels like "psychopath" and "sociopath," will try to hurt you when they feel like they need to in order to get what they want. They can be charming but also manipulative, exploiting your kindness for their own ends, even if it might harm you. Put simply, they do not score high on any of the five dimensions of trust I've previously described.

Wisdom literature in the book of Proverbs refers to these three behavior patterns or groupings as, respectively, wise, foolish, and evil. The wise ones listen to feedback and use it. Conversely, the "fools" hear feedback, but it does no good because they will not own the problem. Proverbs refers to the third category as "evildoers" because they are really, truly destructive and can hurt you badly. So, before attempting a fix, figure out the kind of behavior pattern with which you'll be dealing. A person who can listen, learn, and be coached—that's someone you want on your team, in your family, in your life, since they can mostly get better by learning and showing ownership of the problem.

But what about the ones who won't take feedback? They blame, excuse, and externalize the reasons for their poor performance. So, are they coachable? No, at least not according to the way most of us think of coaching, since they don't think they have a problem. So what do you do? *Help them to have a problem.* It goes something like this:

"Jason, you know how I have talked to you about x, y, or z

and asked you to do things differently? Well, I don't want to talk about those problems anymore. You don't have to worry. I want to talk about a different problem and that is this: I have found that talking to you about problems is not helping. So *that* is the problem I want to address. Is there a way that I can point out issues with you that will help, and you will listen and address the issue in the way that I am expecting? Because if there is not, then I am going to have to protect the business and the team from the consequences of what you are doing or not doing.

"We are at the point where talking more without change cannot continue. I am letting you know that if you cannot agree with me to do x, y, or z, then this is no longer the place for you." Or something to that effect, like "your position will be given to someone else."

Bottom line: When someone is not listening but only blames or makes excuses, then more talking won't help until you hand a new problem to them: The potential negative consequences—a demotion, lower pay, the risk of losing one's job—often gets the wax out of their characterological ears. For the first time, they might have a new thought: "I need to change! Because if I don't, I am going to lose my job." That problem just might get them to move into the wise category. I have seen it happen. You see it anytime an addict gets sober. They didn't own the problem until they got kicked out of the house. They finally have a problem that they are forced, through consequences, to own. But there is an important caveat to this principle: When someone has consistently failed to take ownership of their failures but now announces they will change, you'll need to see verifiable evidence of that change before you bring them back into the fold. They have proven that talking is not worth much. You need to see results that are sustained. (See my book *Trust* for details on how this reconciliation process works.)

Sadly, there is no shortage of people who can't own that they have a problem, even when you bring consequences to the game. Yet to say this fix didn't work isn't altogether accurate, because it *did work*. The fix by your immune system worked. You solved *your* problem. The person's resistance will no longer infect your plan, and you can find a wise person to step into the role. Naturally, you will need to address any legal or HR issues, and you should never let someone go inhumanely, unfairly, or illegally.

Finally, there are the evildoers. Best advice? Go into protection mode. You can't help anyway, and they might try to hurt you. As the rock star Warren Zevon sang, "lawyers, guns, and money" are the tools. You must protect yourself, your people, and the business from someone who is out to destroy you. Talking does not help. Consequences won't get them to see a problem. So, this is where the oft-used sentence came from, "We will only talk to you through our attorney from this point on [the lawyers Zevon refers to]. Here is her number." Or if they may be violent, call the police (guns). And usually, to protect oneself from them costs something (money).

Who says a rock song can't be great leadership training?

Be Available, Not Bombarded

Leaders have a lot to do, but it is a particular *kind* of doing. Looking forward, building vision and strategy, making strategic alliances, culture building, developing leaders, focusing on results, aligning teams to strategy and vision, making sure resources are plentiful, building the bench of talent, satisfying stakeholders, seeing and forming the future, and so on. Often, the leader's work is at a higher altitude than pushing the levers and getting embroiled in operations at a low level. That is why CEOs have COOs and often have presidents. But the same formula holds for every level of leadership. Even if you are not the CEO, you are still responsible for coaching and guiding the individuals on your team. As mentioned, that's why it's important to establish the right cadence for check-ins. But sometimes it can feel like these are taking up all your time, particularly with one person or one team. You long to just say, "Pleeeese go do your work. I am paying you to solve problems, not bring every single dilemma to me." I don't recommend those words, obviously, but here are two ways you might juggle this matter.

One approach is to make the frequency of check-ins a coaching topic. It can be as simple as saying, "Let me share something I have noticed. I find myself having more conversations with you than with the rest of the team. It seems like you need a lot of contact, and I want to explore why. There could be a lot of reasons, but I wanted to understand it from your perspective."

You could go further by offering some possibilities that will reduce the anxiety that the question invites, or just wait for their response. You might say, "For example, I am wondering if our accountability meetings about the plan are providing enough clarity for you. Is there a way we could do better when all together? Is there some way that I am not providing enough clarity? Or I am wondering if the plan is clear enough for you to have the direction you need in the in-between times, like if the activity list is not clear enough. Or does the role or the assignment feel overwhelming to you in some way?"

This kind of query does several things. First, it names the elephant, at least in *your* room. You have brought it to awareness as an issue. Second, it opens the door for exploring solutions. Third, it might give you data that you didn't know, as you learn more from their boots-on-the-ground position. Fourth, you might get a peek into a talent problem, a need for development, or a possible path off the bus. And fifth, it might alert you to a culture problem where people are afraid of making mistakes and are seeking certainty instead of clarity.

The other method is to set a block of time, say Wednesdays from 2:00 to 5:00, when you will hold office hours. Meaning, that is the time that you are available for in-between kinds of help. The best way I have seen this work is when leaders say to the team, "As we implement this plan, things will come up. Of course, if the project is on fire, I need to know. But for many issues that do not carry a big threat that very moment, I can get my work done better if you would just write those down as they occur, make your list, and come see me on Wednesday. That is when I have reserved time for surprise issues or helping you when you need it." You can do it for the whole team, or just that person.

This simple structure puts a boundary up for someone with high inclusion or dependency needs and also provides a safety net for those fearful of making a mistake. If they keep bombarding you with calls for extra attention, you will have discovered the real issue. Just like a parent knows . . . the kid at school who is calling home during the day has some growing up to do.

Embrace Reality

As Scott Peck said in the opening line of *The Road Less Traveled*, which became somewhat of a manual for solving personal problems for the entire culture, for a season decades ago, "Life is difficult." He then goes on to explain that once that reality is accepted, life becomes way less difficult. So much wisdom.

In life and work, reaching a vision is difficult. The road is paved with problems that are screaming to be fixed, getting in between us and our desired futures. If we didn't have problems, we certainly would not need a measurement and accountability function in the human body or in work itself. And since the measurement system would come up empty, we certainly would not need a fix-it system. It would be like having a security system on a house in a zero-crime neighborhood.

But you want to realize your vision, and that can only be done in reality . . . a place where there are problems. As the Woody Allen character Cloquet was described, "He hated reality but realized it was still the only place to get a good steak." It is the *real* world where we have to live.

When you learn to expect problems and normalize them, your brain functions at a higher level. Fewer toxic chemicals are released when an issue occurs, as you are no longer surprised and fighting reality. The fight-flight-or-freeze mode diminishes, and you can skip the drama and solve the problem. Navy SEALs *expect* there to be bad guys on the other side of that wall they are scaling.

Your team starts to think this way, too—as problem solvers, not problem avoiders, or problem victims. A good fix-it system that is part of the culture says to everyone, "Let's go for it. Nothing will stop us." Learn to embrace reality, even when you don't necessarily love what you see.

What About You?

So, we have seen that fixing quickly is key to getting to *there*. Don't let the cavity get so bad that you need a root canal. Let's look at some personal tendencies that you might do well to notice and correct. Consider these your own fix-and-adapt formula.

DO YOU HAVE A HIGH PAIN TOLERANCE?

Sometimes people, because of their backgrounds, develop a sense of over-responsibility for other people's problems and a high tolerance for pain. They might have grown up in a dysfunctional context where pain was the norm. And there was nothing they could do about it, so they learned to shoulder it, do more of the work themselves, be a peacekeeper, and just grin and bear it. This may sound like personal psychobabble, but I have seen high-performing CEOs display this in business. This can also show up as conflict avoidance, which, as we know, increases the chances of a pattern taking root. If you are like that, you might tend to let things go too long, until they become unbearable. Look at yourself and see if you have a long timeline that you let problems remain. Think about the immune system in the human body. It does not wait. It immediately addresses bacteria or infection. Find out what fears or patterns in you keep you from addressing problems before they become infections.

DO YOU TAKE ON OTHER PEOPLE'S PROBLEMS?

Sometimes a parent jumps in and does the homework. Problem fixed, but the next problem is assured. It will happen again. Some leaders will fix and adapt quickly, but they will shoulder the problem themselves, instead of requiring the system, the body to do what it should be doing all along. The popular term for this dynamic is codependent behavior, but it happens in business as well. It is taking on other people's problems when your role is to make sure that they take ownership of the problem and fix it. In terms of the human body, when a muscle group has to take over for another one that is failing, it can lead to new pain and injuries, most likely in the joint or muscle that has been recruited to do the work of a weaker part. Fix the limb that is broken, instead of changing the way you walk.

DO YOU KNOW HOW TO TRIAGE?

If you have ever been in an emergency room, you have noticed that some people who came in after you get seen first. That might be because of triage. Triage is the process of prioritizing patients or conditions based on urgency and the resources that are available. There is a quick assessment, followed by an assignment of priority, whereby they determine if it is life-threatening that requires immediate care, serious but not life-threatening, and up the chain to where it might be real, but is not urgent. It is right-sizing the timeline to the problem.

As you are measuring and holding people accountable, issues arise that require focus. But not all are of the same urgency. And not all are "vital" and might kill you if you don't address them in time. Some people just tend to see all problems as being emergencies, and act as if they are life-threatening, when some of those could be pushed down the "high urgency, high resource allocation, high focus" scale.

Problems will always arise when you are diligently checking into things. But they are not all the same weight. Look at the elements of your plan that should get immediate and/or high resource attention versus those that can wait. You don't want to ignore anything that surfaces from measurement and accountability, since it is in the plan, and you hopefully have already determined that the plan is important. *Everything in the plan is important, or it shouldn't be in there.* But not all are as urgent or weighty as others.

Look at your emotional regulation when there are issues. Do you "emotionally triage"? Or do you hit the flashing lights and sirens at the first sign of danger? Monitor yourself and learn to fix and adapt appropriately, with the right amount of fervor, attention, focus, and resources. Everything is not a life-or-death situation, and we must make sure we do not react as if they are. Some things really are that important, and they need our first attention. That's the reality, too.

Moving Forward

You have seen how the human body reveals what it takes to get from *here* to *there*. You have seen how the five elements—vision, engaging talent, strategy/plan, measurement/accountability, fix/adapt—come together to help you reach your desired future. The path will not always be brightly lit at first, but if you pursue each of these steps, you'll have the tools to make it there, the ability to fix and adapt as you confront new information and new realities.

Conclusion

I was sitting with Finley this morning, having my coffee. She likes to sit with me on the porch, and I love having her there. I was planning my day, and it occurred to me to ask her about her future plans. I asked how she wanted her day to go, what she wanted to experience and accomplish, and at the end of the day, what she would like to look back at and be glad to have done. I also asked how what she did today was going to help her get to where she wanted to be on Thursday.

She looked at me with somewhat of an inquisitive but blank stare that, if it had words, would be "What are you talking about?" At about that time, she heard something at the front door and ran racing to it, like she dutifully does. And then I realized that pretty much *is* her desired future. It is always just doing what she is wired to do, and will continue to do, very well. Past that, she will do it all of her days, just in the ways that she is wired, or any new wiring she gets from training. And, she will enjoy it . . . *Yet, she will never know what it is like to dream of more.*

But, as we have seen, *you* are designed for more. *More* than just continuing to do what you have always done, or in the ways you have always done it, in the ways you are already wired. You are designed, always, for more, because you have the ability to see a desired future for yourself, whether that is short term or long term, in any arena of your life. How you feel, what your relationships look like, and your performance goals.

And, as we have seen, in order to make those visions come to fruition, there is a way that is essential to getting there. And it invites you to first do what Finley can't do, to use the incredible human brain that you have to get above it all, pause, and ask, "What do I want?" Then, once that is clear, to get the players you will need to help, discover the how you will get there, observe how you are doing with each step along the way, and constantly adjust. Any successful endeavor will contain these five elements, and you are capable of putting them all in place. You are literally made to do that, and your brain wants you to!

As we saw in Chapter 1, although you might not have gotten there before or are even discouraged about trying again, there is a good chance that something in that path was missing, and it wasn't necessarily your ability to make it happen. It was just that one or more of these elements required a bit more attention. Do not worry about the past, but be encouraged that the future does not have to be like what you have already experienced. It can be incredibly more, more than you might even be able to fully envision.

My hope for you is that you will be able to grasp that you do *not* have to have all of the gifts or talents within you, or all the resources in the world, to accomplish what you desire. You just need to align yourself with the way that it all works. If you can do that, just embrace the path and put it into action. I truly believe you will see results.

In decades of working with many different kinds of people, from those who start or run global companies, to professional athletes, to people who do more "regular" things, like accomplishing a more desired future in a clinical area, a relationship, or other goals that matter to them, I have seen those seemingly impossible futures realized. And I believe you can do the same.

Remember Jared and his team? Stuck revenue performance for a couple of years in their core, and most cherished business unit? They turned it around, as a handful of years later, it multiplied. They are smart, talented, and tenacious. But remember this, they were all of those things while it was not getting better as well. What changed was they took a deep dive and looked at each element of the way, and got realigned with how a vision gets realized. Today, they still use this path, now expanded to the entire company and its other businesses. And not just to make things better. They have used it to accomplish many vistas, even larger than they were then.

Is it easy? Ha ha . . . ask anyone who has ever accomplished anything of value. Anything of value has value because it is, well . . . valuable. And valuable is never free. It takes work, I won't kid you. Somewhere along the path, as we have seen in many examples in this book, it will be bumpy, sometimes painful. But that is what value costs. It can be painful too.

I could almost sum up the message of this book not as one of avoiding pain—in fact, I call you to embrace some pain. But it is a message of avoiding the kind of pain that *is* avoidable . . . the pain of enduring effort that ends in disappointment, or enduring more pain that is needed because we are not often doing things in the way that will actually work. Not all hard work and effort ends in success, but when it does, one truth stands: People knew what they wanted, had the help they needed, had a way to get there, carefully observed what they were doing along the way, and adjusted themselves and their efforts as they continued. Just like the human body, our teacher here, knows and does better than anyone.

As we saw in each chapter, there will be effort, sometimes invigorating and other times painful. Many times, it is both at the same time! It is not easy to dig deep inside and uncover a dream or desire that has been squashed or held back because of fear or other forces. But boy, can that be energizing! It is not easy to figure out what talent besides our own that we have to engage and bring along with us . . . sometimes it can be very hard to take the risk and ask for that help, even when it is available. But the horizons that open up to us when we do are expansive. Not easy to take the time and curiosity to find the right strategy to get there, even when easier or "tried and true" one is already at our fingertips. But the clarity it brings can turbo charge us. Also, it's hardly ever easy to observe and measure ourselves and then submit to accountability. That is always humbling, and then to take a hard swallow and pivot to fix what is not working is even more humbling and asks for new energy. Yet, the energy it provides outweighs what we spend doing it.

As the old saying goes, to continue to do the same thing expecting different results is not so smart. It works for Finley, but she loves her usual, daily results and never expects or desires a different future tomorrow. She occasionally gets a better future than she has known that day, like when I unexpectedly come home from a great steakhouse with a doggie bag. But I guarantee you that didn't happen because she had envisioned it, sent me out to dinner with a credit card, and made sure the Uber got me home with bag in hand.

For you and me, to continue to do the same thing that got us *here* will not get us to a different *there*. The Thursday that you desire in whatever area of life you want to be better will require some things new, and some things different. My prayer for you is that you continuously, and repeatedly, envision your desired futures, and make them come to pass.

Bless you,
Henry Cloud, PhD
Nashville, TN 2026

Acknowledgments

Acknowledgments are always difficult for me, not because there are not those who should be acknowledged, but because the truth is, for a book like this, there are *so many*. This book is a culmination of decades of learning from many leadership experts, personal mentors, and clients I have worked with. The hands-on experience with clients who implemented these principles has been invaluable to learning *that* they work, and *how* they work. So, if you are anyone on that list, know that I am grateful for you. I wouldn't mention your names anyway ☺.

But a book also has a timeline and path that it is written in, so I am going to mention a few people by name who helped get it done as well:

Shannon Marven and Jan Miller, my agents at Dupree Miller, have been, as always, instrumental. Your guidance, wisdom, great feedback, and joyfulness to work with have been incredible. Thank you for all you did to bring this project to fruition.

Hollis Heimboch, my publisher at HarperCollins, NY, for instant belief in the model, your years of wisdom in business/life writing, and seriously, the best editing I encounter. You made it better.

Greg Bolwer and Albert Adams, for having the patience and

also great encouragement for the content over the many years as we have filmed so many episodes of video presentations of these constructs for our online platforms.

Dave Ramsey, for your strong encouragement over the years about this model.

My wife, Tori, for helping me carve out the time that didn't exist to get it done. Your encouragement keeps me going when there is nothing left in the tank.

The "Bucket Ladies," a small group that took the model and used it so well to accomplish their life visions. You reminded me and showed how this model applies to all areas of life.

My daughter, Lucy, for your early adoption of the model to publish your song "Crash and Learn." You showed its effectiveness and gave us a song that all of us can apply to life.

And finally, Finley, our Doberman. You provided the perfect metaphorical guide for this book. Keep doing what you do so well!

Index

About the Author

Dr. Henry Cloud (www.drcloud.com) is an acclaimed leadership expert, clinical psychologist, and *New York Times* bestselling author. His forty-five books, including the iconic *Boundaries*, have sold nearly 20 million copies worldwide. He has an extensive executive coaching background and experience as a leadership consultant, devoting the majority of his time to working with CEOs, leadership teams, and executives to improve performance, leadership skills, and culture.

Dr. Cloud founded and built a healthcare company, which operated inpatient and outpatient treatment centers in forty markets in the Western United States.

Dr. Cloud's work has been featured and reviewed by *The New York Times*, *The Wall Street Journal*, *The Boston Globe*, *Publishers Weekly*, *Los Angeles Times*, and many other publications. *Success* magazine named Dr. Cloud one of the top twenty-five most influential leaders in personal growth and development alongside Oprah, Brené Brown, Seth Godin, and others. He has been a frequent contributor to CNN, Fox News Channel, and other national media outlets.

As a speaker, he is a favorite at corporate events, conventions, and public arena events on a variety of topics, speaking regularly throughout the United States and internationally.